I0879549

CREEK INDIAN HISTORY

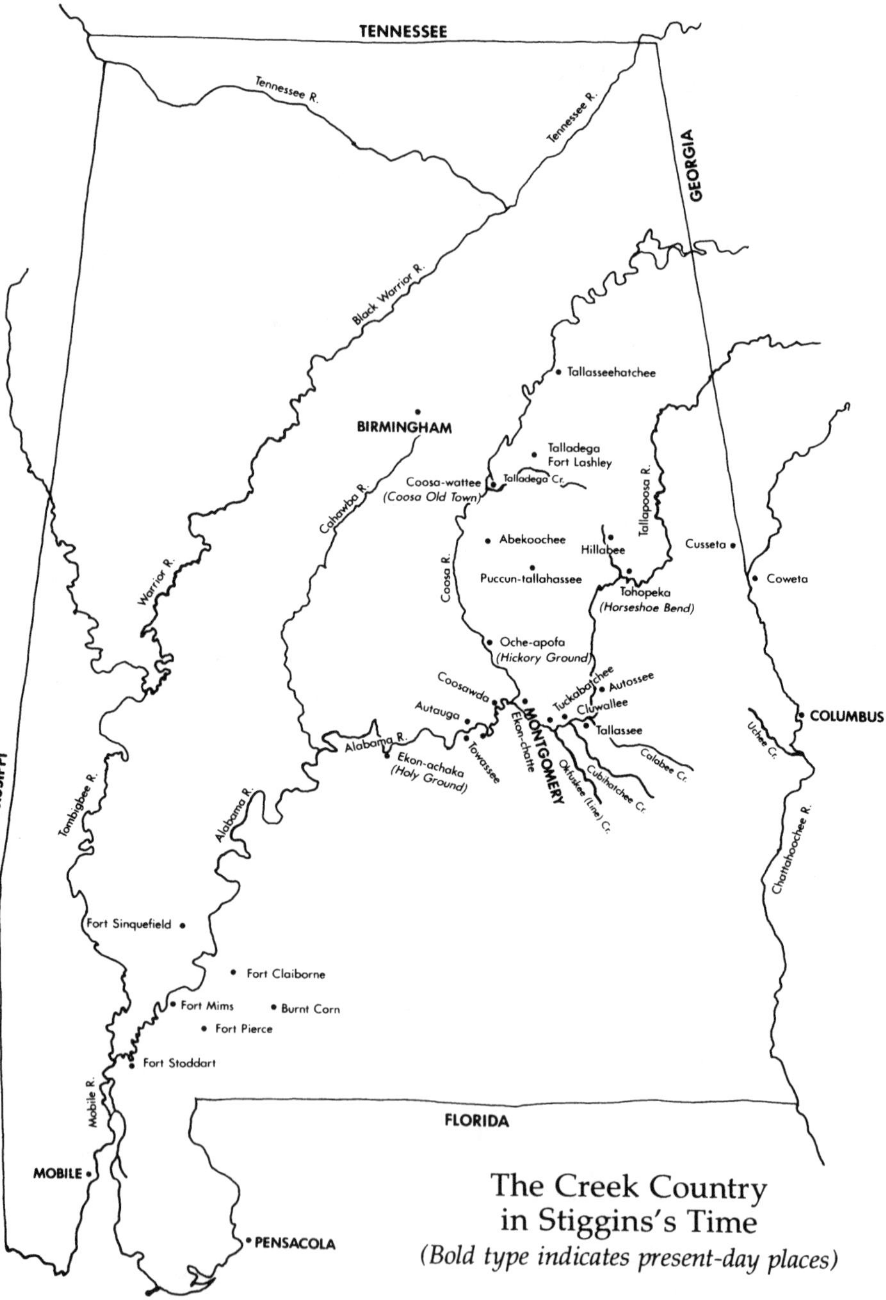

The Creek Country in Stiggins's Time

(Bold type indicates present-day places)

CREEK INDIAN HISTORY

A Historical Narrative of the Genealogy, Traditions and Downfall of the Ispocoga or Creek Indian Tribe of Indians

by One of the Tribe,
GEORGE STIGGINS
(1788-1845)

Introduction and Notes by
WILLIAM STOKES WYMAN
(1830-1915)

Edited by VIRGINIA POUNDS BROWN

Published for the Birmingham Public Library
by The University of Alabama Press

Published for the Birmingham Public Library by
The University of Alabama Press

Printed in the United States of America

Library of Congress Cataloging in Publication Data

Stiggins, George, 1788–1845.
Creek Indian history : a historical narrative of the genealogy, traditions, and downfall of the Ispocoga or Creek Indian tribe of Indians / by George Stiggins; introduction and notes by William Stokes Wyman; edited by Virginia Pounds Brown.
p. cm.
Bibliography: p.
Includes index.
ISBN 0-942301-15-3
ISBN 0-8173-5010-1 (pbk. : alk. paper)
1. Creek Indians—History. 2. Creek Indians—Social life and customs. 3. Indians of North America—Alabama—History. 4. Indians of North America—Alabama—Social life and customs. I. Wyman, William Stokes, 1830–1915. II. Brown, Virginia Pounds. III. Title.
E99.C95S8 1989
976.1'004973—dc20 89-1035

Contents

William Stokes Wyman, front row, is pictured here at the 1912 annual meeting of the Alabama Library Association. To his right is Amelia Gayle Gorgas, librarian, for whom the University of Alabama library is named. Wyman served as acting librarian at the university in the 1870s. Standing, far right, is Thomas M. Owen, director of the Alabama Department of Archives and History, who secured the Stiggins manuscript for Wyman. Other librarians, left to right, are Juliet Hixon, Ora Ioneena Smith, Mary Gorgas.

(Photograph courtesy of WILLIAM STANLEY HOOLE SPECIAL COLLECTIONS LIBRARY, UNIVERSITY OF ALABAMA*)*

Editor's Introduction

George Stiggins, a half-blooded Creek Indian living in Alabama, wrote this history—the only known account by "one of the tribe," as he called himself—150 years ago. It is here printed for the first time in book form. In 1902 its publication seemed imminent. Late that year, Thomas M. Owen, director of the newly created Alabama Archives and History Department, wrote William Stokes Wyman, president of the University of Alabama, that the printer must have Wyman's notes to the Stiggins manuscript by December 1. Wyman replied on December 2:

"I have finished just now the notes (in pencil) on the Stiggins history. Beginning this morning to copy them for the printer I referred to your letter. I find to my surprise that you gave me time to Dec. 1 only.

"I assure you that I devoted to the work all the spare time that I have had to the neglect of everything except my regular college duties. If you can wait till Dec. 15, I feel sure that I can finish the work with an introduction and notes ready for the printer.

"The work has been slow and arduous, because I have had to reexamine so many authorities. The more I have studied Stiggins's relation, the more highly I have appreciated the value of his work.

"If you must have the manuscript now, write or telegraph me at once, and I will send by express immediately. But I am loath to see it go to print without notes" (Wyman to Owen, 2 Dec. 1902. [Ala. Archives and History]).

In spite of Owen's urgency, no published form of the Stiggins manuscript appeared. Wyman's penciled notes and introduction remained with a roughly typed copy of the manuscript in the Alabama Archives and History Department, Montgomery, Alabama. It was here that the present editor discovered the material while researching southeastern Indian history. With the increased interest today in native Americans and the paucity of firsthand information about Indians of the Southeast, particularly about the Creeks, the need for Stiggins's unique work to be published was evident. Included in this edition are Wyman's introduction and notes, major contributions to the value of the book. Also included are editor's notes, based on newer sources not available to Wyman.

William Stokes Wyman (1830-1915) was, in his time, considered Alabama's leading authority on the Indian tribes who had lived in the state. He was not only knowledgeable about Indian history but well versed in the languages of the Choctaws and the Creeks. He wrote articles about southern Indians for such magazines as *The Nation, Century,* and *Magazine of American History.* Wyman's special interest lay in early explorations of the Southeast as they related to the Indians. This interest led him to extensive research and collecting in Spanish and French, as well as British and American, sources. His facility with languages served him well, as many sources now available in English had not been translated from the French and Spanish in his day. His notes reflect the diversity of his sources and his scholarly concern for facts concerning Alabama Indians.

(Wyman's reputation in Alabama rests not on his Indian knowledge but on his fifty-six years of distinguished service to the University of Alabama. He joined the faculty in 1852, one year after his graduation, to teach Latin. He became a noted classical scholar, teaching both Latin and Greek and producing a Latin grammar. Even though he preferred to teach, he served as acting president of the university four times, refusing the presidency until 1901. He resigned the presidency a year later and continued to teach until his retirement in 1908.)

Wyman had tried to locate the Stiggins manuscript long before Owen placed a copy in his hands. In 1873, Wyman tells us in his story of the manuscript (see Introduction by Wyman), he asked a fellow faculty member, Thomas C. McCorvey, to contact the Stiggins family, which he did, only to discover that Lyman Draper, secretary of the State Historical Society of Wisconsin, had taken the papers to examine for possible purchase. Later, Wyman apparently contacted Wisconsin sources without success. It remained for Thomas M. Owen, the young and vigorous director of the Alabama Archives and History Department, to locate the manuscript in the Wisconsin archives. Draper, an insatiable but erratic collector of frontier Americana, had kept his collection in disarray in his personal library. At his death, his collection was taken to the Wisconsin State Historical Society and recatalogued and classified. The Stiggins manuscript may well have been "lost" in Draper's collection in the intervening years.

In 1897 the secretary of the Wisconsin State Historical Society recommended one of his employees, Georgiana R. Sheldon, to copy in longhand the 156 pages of the manuscript. Sheldon agreed to copy the work "for 32 to 35 dollars." She wrote: "I am using the utmost pains in copying the spelling, but you will find [Stiggins] is not at all consistent in it, spelling a name often two or three different ways on a page. I have followed the manuscript exactly in this matter, also in punctuation which is very faulty." She was paid $34.20 for her work.

Sheldon's transcribed copy became part of the Alabama archives on April 27, 1901. Owen either had a typed copy made from the longhand copy for Wyman's use, or Wyman typed his own working copy. He made additions and corrections in pencil as he checked it against the original transcription.

In the years since Wyman's work, the Stiggins manuscript has continued to be recognized as important source material for Creek Indian history. John R. Swanton, dean of southeastern anthropology, considered Stiggins a highly useful primary source for his *Early History of the Creek Indians* and quoted extensively from him. Frank Owsley, who edited the 1969 reprint of Halbert and Ball's *The Creek War of 1813 and 1814*, first published in 1895, found Stiggins most valuable in evaluating the work of Halbert and Ball. "The significant fact," Owsley wrote, "is that the two accounts are very similar. They differ on a few points, but . . . their similarity obviously strengthens the claim of both accounts to accuracy" (xii).

In 1933 Peter Brannon, Indian historian, later to become director of the Alabama Archives and History Department, wrote in *Alabama Highways* about "the celebrated

Stiggins attended the Cubihatchee Baptist Church—which still stands today near Shorter, Alabama—and is buried in an unmarked grave in the church cemetery. He was living on a nearby farm when he wrote his history. (Photograph by JOHN HOLT*)*

manuscript.'' Brannon said that Stiggins compiled his history while he was living in the heart of Creek country, a short distance from Montgomery, near present-day Shorter. His farm, between Cubihatchee and Line Creeks, bordered the old federal road, a thoroughfare for Indian travel both before and after the white man came. Passing along information provided by Stiggins's son, Brannon wrote that Stiggins was stout, weighing 220 pounds, and short, five feet six inches. ''He ate but little, slept but little, read much and was blessed with a retentive memory.''

Brannon stated that Stiggins attended the Cubihatchee Baptist Church and is buried in an unmarked grave in the cemetery there. Since Stiggins served with the Americans in the Creek War, Brannon proposed to solicit a headstone from the U. S. quartermaster general so ''future travelers may see that here George Stiggins's bones are resting.''

The editor visited the Cubihatchee cemetery and found no evidence of such a marker.

Wyman elected to leave the manuscript unedited ("bad grammar, bad spelling, and all"). In this publication basic editing has been done to the frequently obscure and wordy manuscript in the interest of clarity and readability. Punctuation and spelling have also been corrected. Neither Stiggins nor Wyman was consistent in the spelling of proper names; for example, Stiggins spells *Tuckabatchee* four ways, Wyman spells it three ways. After consulting many sources, the editor has standardized the spellings of tribes, towns, and individuals in both the Stiggins manuscript and Wyman's notes. Stiggins used some headings; the editor has added others to clarify the text.

This publication is based on a photocopy of the typed text used and corrected by Wyman. The editor has checked it against a microfilm of Stiggins's longhand original, a process which revealed a few important copyist omissions and other errors. The microfilm on file in the Linn-Henley Research Library of the Birmingham Public Library is part of the Lyman Draper Manuscript Collection (Georgia, Alabama, and South Carolina papers, series V, vol. 1, from State Historical Society of Wisconsin).

The work would not have been possible without the expertise of Laurella Owens, who served as copy editor and consultant. The editor is indebted also to the Alabama Archives and History Department; to Mary Bess Paluzzi and Yvonne Crumpler of the Linn-Henley Research Library staff; to Elizabeth Wells, librarian of the Special Collections at Samford University; to Joyce Lamont, William Stanley Hoole Special Collections Library, University of Alabama; and to Margaret Miller and John Holt.

Wyman's Introduction

"The Historical Narrative of the Ispocoga or Creek Tribe of Indians" here presented to the public was written by George Stiggins, a half-blood of the Natchez tribe. Although left in an unfinished state, it is an important addition to our knowledge of this interesting people and to the history of Alabama.

"The brave natives of Alabama had no writers among them to record their achievements." This is the wise and truthful remark of Albert J. Pickett, author of a history of Alabama. We have now in Stiggins's work an account of many of the scenes and events of the Creek War of 1813, from the standpoint of the Indians.

Born in the heart of the Creek nation, connected by blood and marriage with many of the active participants in the battles that were fought, Stiggins had opportunities that no white man could have had of getting the real facts of the history of those troubled times. The interest which attaches to this document, now for the first time printed, after lying in manuscript for more than fifty years, is all the greater because it bears throughout the marks of an honest endeavor to reach the truth and faithfully record it. Much of the romance of the history of Alabama will now disappear in the clear white light of

Stiggins's homely but truthful narrative.

A Sketch of the Author's Life. The facts embraced in the following brief sketch are derived in part from letters written to Lyman C. Draper, sometime secretary of the Wisconsin Historical Society, by the late W. R. Maiben of Monroe County, Alabama, who lived near Stiggins in the early days and was intimately acquainted with him; but mainly from letters written to Draper by Joseph N. Stiggins of Mount Pleasant, Monroe County, who is a son of George Stiggins. These letters are now deposited in the archives of the Wisconsin Historical Society at Madison, Wisconsin.

For copies of these letters and also for a copy of the manuscript of the history I am indebted to the kindness of Thomas M. Owen, the tireless and faithful director of the Department of Archives and History for Alabama. Mr. Owen has taken the pains to have fair copies made of the manuscript and the correspondence, and these are now deposited in the archives of the Department in the capitol at Montgomery.

George Stiggins was born in the Talladega region of Alabama in the year 1788, not far from the spot on which the present town of Talladega is built. His father, Joseph Stiggins, of English descent, was born near Roanoke River in Virginia, and came to the Creek country during the Revolutionary War. He conducted a trade between the Indians and the Spaniards of Florida. While engaged in this business he married a full-blooded woman of the Natchez tribe, a widow whose English name was Nancy Grey. Her Indian name has not been handed down.

She and her two sisters who likewise married white

William Stokes Wyman
(Photograph courtesy of WILLIAM STANLEY HOOLE SPECIAL COLLECTIONS LIBRARY, UNIVERSITY OF ALABAMA*)*

men, were nieces of Chinnabe, principal chief of the Natchez tribe. It must be remembered that a remnant of the Natchez, after the destruction of the tribe in 1729 by the French, removed to the Creek nation and had established themselves in the Talladega valley fifty years before the close of the Revolutionary War. The principal town of the Natchez was situated on the Tallasseehatchee Creek, ten miles above its junction with the Coosa. George Stiggins, by the Natchez law of descent, might have succeeded, if he had wished, to the chieftainship of the tribe.

About the year 1800, Joseph Stiggins removed with his family to the Tensaw River near Mobile. His home was within a mile of the parallel of 31 degrees, which was the boundary line at that time between the Spanish and American possessions in this quarter, probably in the neighborhood of Stockton in Baldwin County.

Joseph Stiggins was called a well educated man for the times and region in which he lived. Besides his knowledge of English, he had a colloquial acquaintance with Spanish, and with the Creek, Cherokee, and Natchez languages. He gave his children the best education possible in that region so remote from the ways of civilization, fetching teachers from Mobile and elsewhere to train them at home.

In this way George acquired what was called a good practical English education, and learned something of Latin besides. He understood the Creek and Natchez languages, the latter being literally his mother tongue; but he could speak neither with fluency. In later years he acquired a colloquial knowledge of Spanish through frequent business intercourse with the Spaniards of Florida.

In the year 1810, when he had hardly reached manhood, young Stiggins, impelled by the spirit of adventure, joined the wild expeditions of the Kempers, organized to wrest Mobile from the Spaniards; but his father brought him off safely from this rash undertaking before the expedition came to a disastrous end. In 1812 he was happily married to a young lady of the white race—Miss Elizabeth Adcock of the Mississippi Territory. When the Creek War began, since his father was a white man, his wife a white woman, and his two Natchez aunts had both married white men, he felt it to be his duty to go with the white people, as most of the half-bloods did. Yet he was not void of sympathy for his unfortunate and misguided kinsmen of the red race. At the time of the assault on Fort Mims, Stiggins was a member of the half-breed Dixon Bailey's company of volunteers under Major Daniel Beasley, the commanding officer of the fort. Providentially, he was absent from the fort at the time of the massacre. On that fateful day, August 31, 1813, he was in Mobile on furlough, and thus probably escaped death. His sister, Mrs. Susan Stiggins Hathaway, was in the fort. Her husband was killed, but Mrs. Hathaway was saved by Efa Tustenuggee, the Dog Warrior of Autossee, one of the hostile band.

At the close of the Creek War, Stiggins established himself as a farmer at Mount Pleasant in Monroe County. In 1817 his sister Mary married William Weatherford, the Red Eagle, the reputed leader of the Creeks in the late war. In the neighborhood of Mount Pleasant Stiggins lived until he was appointed in 1830 a special agent of the Creek nation. He was present in Washington in 1832 when the Creek treaty for the removal of the Indians from Alabama to the Indian Territory was concluded. While engaged in business for the nation he visited his two old Natchez aunts in the Talladega country. "When the old king of the Natchez came into his presence" [his son recalled], "after the usual ceremonies, he seated himself, crossing his legs, it being customary for the old king to assume this attitude in the presence of his successors." But Stiggins, not caring to be counted as the Great Sun of the Natchez tribe, declined the honorable office.

In 1831 Stiggins removed to Macon County and operated a farm between Line and Cubihatchee Creeks. Here he spent in retirement the remainder of his useful and eventful life. It was here that he wrote his History of the Creeks. His son Joseph N. Stiggins mentioned that his father had from early manhood kept a diary of important historical events. This diary, which would be of high historical value, now has unfortunately been lost. In his last illness Stiggins expressed deep regret that he had not been able to complete the History. He died of dropsy of the chest November 22, 1845, and was followed to the grave by a large concourse of sorrowing friends. He lies buried in the graveyard of the old Cubihatchee Baptist Church in Macon County. His grave is unmarked by any stone, and there is probably no one now living who can point out his last resting place.

"Stiggins abounded," says his old friend W. R. Maiben, "in anecdote[s] of the most varied character. His great fluency of speech and geniality of manner gave an interest to everything that he uttered. He was entirely simple and unpretending. General Jackson, the massacre at Mims, the warrior Weatherford and his recent death were all subjects of his conversation. A pair of lively and expressive black eyes and a round, good-humored face intensified the enjoyment of his really eloquent and facile words in narrative."

The Story of the Manuscript. Internal evidence shows that much if not all of this Historical Narrative was written by Stiggins prior to the forcible removal of the Creeks from Alabama in 1836. After Stiggins's death the manuscript was preserved with great care by his widow for many years. Albert J. Pickett, who published his *History of Alabama* in 1851, was allowed once, while he was engaged in collecting material for his work, to examine the manuscript for an hour. This fact he mentions in the preface to his book. Elsewhere he expresses an unfavorable critical judgment on the merits of Stiggins's work.

The writer of these notes made an unsuccessful effort in the year 1873 to purchase the manuscript. In the summer of that year, Professor T. C. McCorvey of the University of Alabama, who is a native of Monroe County, at the request of this writer, kindly consented to visit the Mount Pleasant neighborhood, where the descendants of Stiggins were then living, with the hope of finding the manuscript and contracting for its purchase. He ascertained and regretfully reported that the precious document was then in the hands of Lyman C. Draper, secretary of the Wisconsin Historical Society, who had borrowed it with a view to purchase. Mr. Draper having died after this, application was made to his successor in office to ascertain whether the Wisconsin Historical Society had made the purchase of the interesting relic. Answer was made that the officers of the society knew nothing of the document. The search was then abandoned. Finally Mr. Owen, the accomplished director of the Department of Archives and History for Alabama, who holds a brevet for finding anything that is likely to increase our store of information relating to the history of Alabama, having ascertained that the manuscript was beyond doubt in the possession of the Wisconsin Historical Society, had a fair copy made which is now deposited among the Alabama collections.

Stiggins was wholly unversed in the art of literary composition; but his narrative bears throughout the stamp of scrupulous regard for the truth of history. In preparing the work for publication I have preferred to leave the text as I found it, bad spelling, bad grammar and all. I have corrected only a few obvious mistakes of the copyist, and altered the punctuation, so as to make the content clear and intelligible to the reader.

In writing the notes, wherever I have had occasion to cite other authors, I have for the most part referred to the ultimate authorities, that is to say, to the original and oldest sources of information. The statements of second-hand writers have been adopted only when they seem to conform to these older evidences.

A HISTORICAL NARRATIVE

of the Genealogy, Traditions and Downfall of the Ispocoga or Creek Indians

Stiggins's Preface

It is entirely through the solicitations of many of my friends who were excited by curiosity to know somewhat more of the Creek Indians than they could hear or see about them that I have been induced to compile a historical narrative of that body. I do assure you, my gentle reader, that it has been with a degree of hesitation that I have commenced trying a public exposition of the traditional history and genealogy of my woe-worn and pitiable country. . . .

I wish it to be taken into consideration that I undertake this work as a man hoodwinked; that I have not, nor do I see, any material from which to form or produce a narrative. I wish it further observed that I have not the chance of a man who takes a pen in hand to write on a well-known subject, nor of him who has a chance to read and extract from approved and studied history. Guided and assisted by either of the aforesaid cases, I would have no hesitation of mind to proceed on the subject. . . .

I shall have fables and traditions in many cases to surmount, and but few to recount; for the traditions of the Indians have been handed down through generations more as instruction than as information to elucidate the inquiring mind. I have been in and participated in their debates in council and know the strength, information, and power of mind that the present chiefs possess. I have never heard any of them traditionally say or suppose that the principal tribe had any origin but here; so they hold no tradition of emigration from any country that I ever heard.[1] But regarding such branches of the national body that I know of who derived their origin elsewhere, I shall relate the traditional account of their settlement and union with the Ispocoga body.[2] As it is a matter not common to find an Indian with antiquated curiosities, he will seldom ask a man more than his business and residence. Many more questions to an Indian are, in his estimation, idle curiosity and impertinence. So it will happen, the more a stranger questions an Indian, the less pains he will take to abide by the truth in his information. When travelers through their nation . . . ask the one question least known to the Indians, that is, where the Indians originally resided, what direction or quarter of the world they came from, and emphatically repeat these questions, the Indian, in order to rid himself of impertinent importunity, . . . recounts a fabricated tale as a tradition not heard before, by himself or anyone else, invented merely to suit his auditors, which tale said auditors will tell as a national tradition. So there are ever new traditions for the curious and inquisitive traveler. In order to steer clear of such a labyrinth of paradoxes I shall take the most probable side of that I have heard them relate, when I can, and seek for more.

I can assert that it is not known by the Indians why the present assemblage of their tribes came by the appellation of Muscogee,[3] whether the Muscogee aborigines were destroyed or became extinct in the present tribes and only left their name at their extinction; for the present Creek or Muscogee body is composed of the following tribes who retain their primitive tongues and customs: the Alabamas, Hitchitees, Uchees, Puccunnas, Abekas, Ispocogas, Natchez. These tribes are inseparably united by compact and consolidated by individual and national interest. I shall take the tribes both separately and bodily in detail with their form of government, religious customs and manners, and the most prominent parts of their history to their downfall with an explanatory vocabulary of persons, names, rivers, animals, etc.

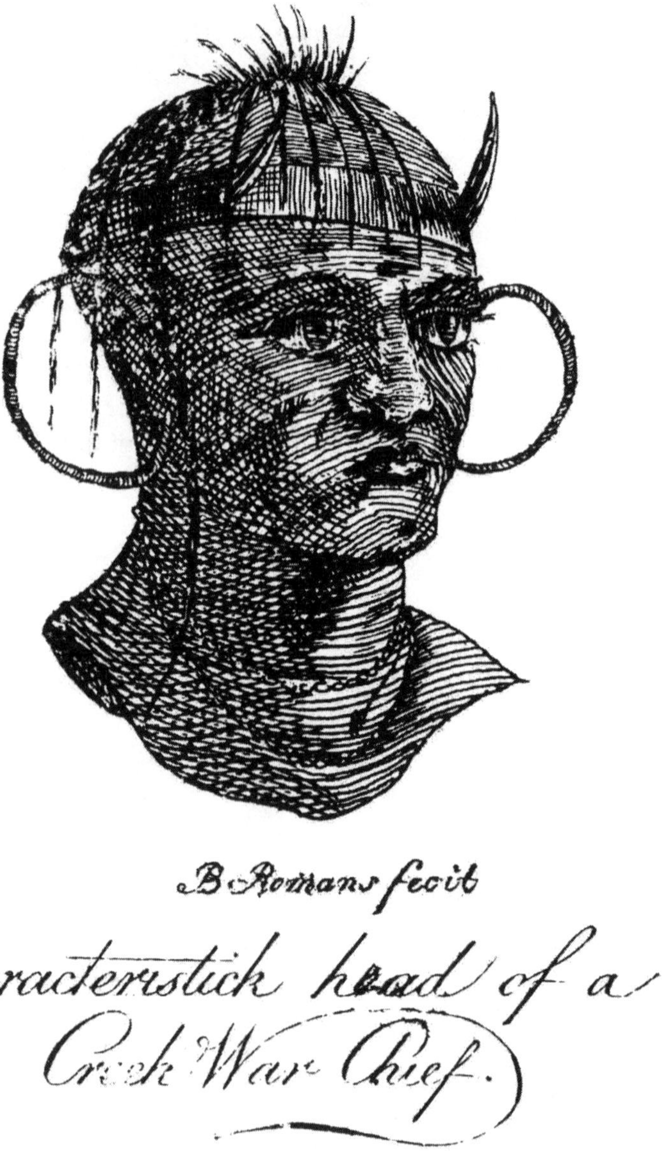

Bernard Romans, Dutch engraver, surveyor, and botanist, made this drawing of a Creek war chief about 1755.
(Photograph courtesy of SMITHSONIAN INSTITUTION, BUREAU OF AMERICAN ETHNOLOGY*)*

TRIBES AND GOVERNMENT

Tribes

Alabamas

The first settlement we find in tracing the Alabamas (a branch of the Creek or Iscopoga tribe) is at the confluence of the Alabama River and Tensaw Lake near the town of Stockton in Baldwin County.

Their settlements extended up the lake and river as far as Fort Mims. Their town sites and other settlements they called Towassee, and at this time they call that extent of country Towassee Tallahassee which is "Towassee Old Town."[4] The white settlers of the place call it Tensaw settlement. The Indians say traditionally that at the time of their residence there they were a very rude, barbarous set of people and in a frightful state of ignorance. Their missile weapons for both war and subsistence were bows and arrows made of cane and pointed with flint or bone sharpened to a point. With the same weapons they repelled their foe in time of war. In the winter time they got their subsistence in the forest, and they made use of [the weapons] to kill the fish in the shallow parts of the lakes in the summer season.

They say very jocosely they consider that at this time were they to meet one of their ancestors armed in ancient manner and dressed in buckskin of his own manufacture that it would inspire them with dread to behold his savage appearance. They very often make mention of their forefathers of that age, calling it the time when their ancestors made an inhuman appearance, by which we may judge that the then state of their forefathers has been handed down to them as a very rude and frightful state almost beyond conception. They do not pretend to any traditional account, when or for what they emigrated to this distance. They have a tradition that many of the inhabitants of ancient Towassee for some reason unknown to them were carried off on shipboard by the French or some other white people many years since. It must have been in consequence of said interruption when the Towassee settlement was depopulated and carried off on shipboard that the remainder of the tribe removed up the river and made the settlements of the towns Autauga and Towassee in the bend of the river below the city of Montgomery. They resided there till the close of their hostile movements in the year 1813.[5] After the Treaty of Fort Jackson and the cession of their country, they moved up the Tallapoosa where their number at this time would be about two thousand in three settlements: one above the mouth of the creek called Autauga, one above the mouth of Cubihatchee called Towassee, the other on the Coosa River in a town called Oche-ap-ofa or Hickory Ground.[6]

They call their tribe Alabama, but by other tribes they are mostly called Che-loke-cul-ga,[7] which is "a man that uses an imperfect or mixed language."

The greatest evidence, in my opinion, of their antiquated residence in this state is the river bearing their name. [It is called the Alabama] among all the other tribes of the national body from the junction of the Coosa and Tallapoosa Rivers to its junction with Tensaw Lake at the town of Stockton. As it is common for Indians to note or name a thing after any uncommon occurrence, I make no hesitation in saying that the Alabamas were found here by the other tribes when they located themselves here, and they named the river Alabama after them in acknowledgment of their antiquity.[8]

As the present tribe of Alabamas have no tradition of origin or derivation,[9] it raises a presumption in my mind that they had a connection at some distant period with the Chickasaw or Choctaw tribes, most probably with the latter. I may say consequently that they are a relic of the Choctaw tribe from two other concurrent sources. First is the similarity of the tongues. No doubt the mongrelizing of the tongues occurred as a result of the connection of the Alabamas with the Creek tribe; the Alabamas had no grammatical rule to retain their language in its original style or purity. Second, they had so extensive a settlement and land claim, without competition of the other tribes, for a distance of nearly five hundred miles, and they had no traditional idea of any other place where there are so many mounds for the disposal of their dead. This was the original method of disposing of the dead among the Choctaws, and is still partially practiced among them to this day. Though the Alabamas of this time do not practice this mode with their dead, they may have quit it since their assimilation with the Creek body, as it was singular to the modes of burial in the other tribes.[10]

In all national concerns and public assemblies the Alabama head men have the standing and voice that the chiefs of the others tribes have. While in the assemblies they use the Creek tongue; in their local concerns they use their own tongue or language. They are tenacious of their private self-government, seldom associating with any other Indians. The tongue they speak is similar to and can be understood by the Choctaws, Chickasaws, Hitchitees, and Coosawdas, which five bodies in time may have been one nation detached by some circumstance and separated finally.[11] The Alabamas are generally very honest in their dealing and are an inoffensive body of people with but few exceptions, being men of sterling courage in general. They manifested this by the enterprise and damage they did to the white settlements down the river; for they did more murder and other mischief in the time of their hostilities in the year 1813 than all the other tribes together. They have no manner of worship nor no ideas of performing or practicing any adoration to a supreme being other than in thanksgiving for the new crop of corn, which they do annually in a very devout and reverent manner.[12] They believe in a supreme disposer of fate, for they are predestinarians, always consoling themselves for any misfortune by saying it was so ordered by the great man above.

About the year 1793 there was an old Coosawda chieftain called Red Shoes who was violently opposed to their making war on the Chickasaws. As it was determined contrary to his will, he resolved to quit the nation, so he and a mulatto man who resided with the Alabamas named Billy Ashe headed a party of about twenty families, part Coosawdas and the rest Alabamas. They moved to the Red River and tried a settlement about sixty miles up from its mouth. But on trial they were so annoyed and infested by small red ants that were numerous in that country that they found it hardly possible to put anything beyond the ants' reach or destruction. So after living there a few years they removed finally from thence to the province of Texas on the River Trinity, a few miles from the mouth of said river where they now live.[13]

Uchees

The first we know of the Uchees, who are this day a part of the Ispocoga body, was that once, according to tradition, they were natives of the state of Georgia living on part of the Ogeechee called Uchee Creek, which may go by that name yet. That place is about as far as their residence can be traced.[14]

They were no doubt the most savage of all the tribes, which caused their removal and settlements on the Big and Little Uchee Creeks below Girard in the state of Alabama. Their savage and wild disposition was undoubtedly the reason they continually receded as the settlements of white people approached them. They can prove a neighborship at some distant day to the Shawanose who resided about Savannah at the time the Uchees did on Ogeechee. Both tribes may have quit their abode on the colonization of Georgia by General Oglethorpe about a century ago in Savannah where the Shawanose then resided. But as the Uchees could not behold a land of agriculture and civilization, they gradually receded from their fastness and haunts. They at length united their destiny with the tribe of Muscogee under whose nurturing hand they bask in the pleasure of freedom. They are more entitled than any other tribe in the Creek nation to the appellation of the son of the forest, being attached to a life of sauntering and lounging and camping in the uninhabited parts of the wilderness.

The Uchees are worse than the other tribes of the nation in many things, if possible, being more indolent, more thievish, more dissipated, and depraved in their morals. They are ever in feud with the other Indians for their thefts and other depredations of a prowling nature. From their unsettled disposition they have very few towns of residence, and, of course, few farms.

Though they are considered as of the Ispocoga body, they are a perfectly independent people. No cognizance is being taken of their actions or manners by the other tribes of the nation. Their dishonesty is proverbial in the nation, so that any remarkable thief is said to be like an Uchee, licensed to steal with impunity.[15] In all conversations among themselves or not they speak their own barbarous tongue, which is a quick guttural stammering accent not very unlike the dying respiration of an old sow under the hands of a butcher. The Uchee tongue is only spoken by the natives of the tribe as there are no more than four or five instances of its being learned and spoken by anyone else. They are so attached to their own tongue and mode of living that very few of them make any use of or can converse in the national tongue. This is said by the other tribes of the nation to be owing to the general dislike expressed and manifested among them, as well as to their wild, roguish, and inspired nature.[16]

Puccunnas

The Puccunnas at this day are only known by tradition to have been a distinct people and their ancient town or habitation is called Puccun-tallahassee, which is Puccun Old Town. This ancient town is in the present Coosa country of the state of Alabama. The Abekas have a tradition that the Puccunnas were a distinct people and that they in old times were very numerous. They do not say whether they were emigrants or not, or at what time they became one of the national body; but they say, as they belonged to the national body one and inseparable, there was no distinction made, so by continual intermarriage with the other tribes they at length became absorbed and assimilated with their neighbors without distinction. No other knowledge is left regarding them but the name of their ancient habitation. Whether in conversation they had a separate tongue of their own, tradition is silent.[17]

Abekas

The Abeka tribe reside indiscriminately in the Talladega Valley with the Natchez tribe, whom they admitted to locate and assimilate with their tribe as one people indivisible a little more than a century ago. They at this day only pretend to know and distinguish their tribes from the mother's side of descent, but they are as one people with the Natchez at this time.

Tribes Described by Stiggins

The Abekas of this day are no doubt the lineal descendants of the people who somewhat more than three centuries past so unavailingly and violently opposed the adventurous Ferdinand Soto in his researches through their country, according to the first historical account we have of them.[18] They may by conjecture be entitled to the claim of the primitive Muscogee more than any other of the tribes, for they are not discriminated by any ancient denomination that is known of.

Their appellation is derived from their manner of approving a proposition. Though the national tongue is spoken by the tribe in all its purity, it must be noted that they assent or approbate what you may say to them in conversation with the long aspiration *aw*, whereas the rest of the nation approbate or answer short *caw*. From their manner of answering they got the name Abeka. Moreover, the rest of the Indians in talking of them and their tongue aptly call it Abeka tongue and never resort to the appellation of Ispocoga, only in the national way.[19]

The Abeka part of the tribe inhabiting the valley of Talladega are lineally descended from the people visited by Ferdinand Soto of Spain in his researches for gold among the tribes in about the year 1515.[20] From the transcript of peregrination he has left it is evident that the Abekas had been residents for a length of time previous to that date. I will put a query to the reader with a combination of circumstances for his own conjecture and solution. Soto says he was as far north as Nickajack in the Cherokees, which was so named at that distant time, and of passing through Coosa-wattee, which name in the Cherokee language is Coosa Old Town.[21] He further mentions in the vicinity of his Abekoochee fortification a town called Coosa Tul-muchessee,[22] which in the Creek, or Abeka, tongue is Coosa New Town, which stands near the banks of the Coosa River; at this time it is called Kelly's Town.

At what era the Abekas resided in Coosa-wattee and why they moved and why they built Coosa Tul-muchessee, tradition is silent. But many would say with myself that the Abekas once resided in Coosa-wattee, from whence they were expelled by the Cherokees. After their expulsion they made their location in Talladega Valley on the river, and named their new town in remembrance of their former abode, Coosa Tul-muchessee, or Coosa New Town. I shall make a conjecture that from the aforesaid two towns Coosa River originated its name.

So, gentle reader, I have made all my references as a query and put them before you so you can consider with me. The town of Abekoochee in the Talladega Valley would raise an inference that there was or had been a larger town of that name somewhere, for that name in English is Little Abeka. Whether they had a larger town of that name or why they should so name the town, tradition is silent and I am unable to say.[23] Ferdinand Soto further says that he had a fortified camp near the last named town, which I suspect may be relied on as a fact; for, in the vicinity of the town on the margin of a large boiling spring, the ruins of a breastwork that appears to be of an antique date are visible.[24] While Soto remained in said breastwork he says he was attacked by the natives of the place several times. At that time the Indians may have taken a brass drum that was in their possession not a half-century ago, kept as a trophy and said by them to have been got by their ancestors in times of old from a people who invaded or passed in a hostile manner through their country coming from up the river.[25] The Indians said they were not like any people they ever saw before, that they were ferocious, proud, and impudent in their manners. From the traditional circumstance of the brass drum it would lead to the inference that the proud people alluded to were the escort of Ferdinand Soto, and that the Indians came in possession of one of his drums by some means. Most probably he was attacked at the place by the whole nation when and where they may have got possession of six brass trappings or breastplates held in superstitious veneration by the Tuckabatchees. Of them I will speak hereafter.

Soto makes mention again of encamping near the junction of the two rivers and names the place Mavillas[26] where the Indians attacked him several times in large bodies. When they found themselves unable to make an impression on his camp, they came to terms of peace. I merely infer as I said before that remarkable adventures or circumstances would aptly derive a name of note, so the aforesaid attack and peace may have transpired at an ancient breastwork on the rising ground nearly opposite the creek near the Othlewallee, called by the white people Cluwallee,[27] as the name of that town is Division of War, or Where They Fought and Parted. What other notable transaction could have merited a town of that name I cannot divine, for I have inquired of men of that town who I thought had some tradition of that among many others they could relate, but got no clue to alter the above advanced conjecture. So I shall leave it to the next better informed commentator to solve, and proceed to the Natchez tribe.

Natchez

The men of the Natchez tribe almost all converse in the Creek tongue, with their families or not. Though the women can speak it fluently, yet most generally in their own common concerns and to their children they use their own native tongue. Frequently in one house they use both tongues without any detriment to their conversation or business.[28]

The tradition the Natchez relate as the cause of their removal from the seat of their nativity to their final settlements in the Talladega Valley I will relate as I heard it. About one century ago the tribe lived in one large body or tribe town on the bank of the Mississippi where the present city of Natchez now stands and extended above it. Their government was monarchical; all cases both civil and political were determined by the king and his suite, for he was attended by both men and women in great style. The throne was hereditary and the king was supreme head of the tribe. His person was sacred and his mandates inviolable. He lived in a retired manner in the suburbs of the town, secluded from the society of all persons but his own near relations, who officiated about his person, both men and women, as attendants and guards. About one third of his connection at a time, and such as were not in attendance on his person, were in the forest in search of game for his subsistence. During the hunting excursion the party was headed by one of his near relatives to direct and take care of the party.

But it must be noticed that all earthly institutions, though made for lasting happiness for ages, are delusive and visionary. So it happened to them. For while they were living under the peaceable and happy institution of government (a government familiarized to them by time, and consonant to their habits of life), they received a visit from a detachment of French who went up the Mississippi to explore the country and fix on an eligible spot to erect a garrison. Without a previous compact with the natives to insure their good will, they pitched on a site in the vicinity of the town, though much against the will of the Indians. The Natchez disguised their chagrin and seemingly were careless and not opposed to the encroachments of their unwelcome visitants and neighbors, who had fortified themselves in the suburb below the town.

The French, by their gallantry, pursued the destructive

course said to have been in Sodom of olden time. As though danger was not imbruing, nor destruction awfully pending over their ill-fated heads, they made free with the men and married the women. The natives tolerated their love to the women with seeming good will, for they saw the advantage that would ultimately result. The Frenchmen's blind devotion to love would make them unsuspicious and unguarded against a design they had in contemplation. As was expected, their lewd practices soon caused a relaxation in their vigilance and discipline, for they frequented the town at night in a careless manner and unguardedly admitted the women into the fortress at night and made them welcome visitants at all times. The Indians saw how remiss and negligent the French were getting in their manner of living, and they for revenge secretly and exultingly proceeded to put their scheme in execution, which was to exterminate their gallant and unwelcome neighbors. The Indian men concerted a plan with their women, for the women to make their appointment with the Frenchmen to be within the fortress on such a night. When the time arrived, instead of the expected women, the fortress was entered by men in disguise and armed, who instantly fell to work and exterminated the whole garrison of men. One man escaped because his loving wife, wishing to save him, had prevailed on him to stay with her in the town that night, and after the above catastrophe she effected his escape down the river Mississippi. So he carried the news to his countrymen of the disaster to his comrades.

The Indians were very much elated with the success of their plan, which had exceeded even their most sanguine expectations, getting clear of their intruders so quickly

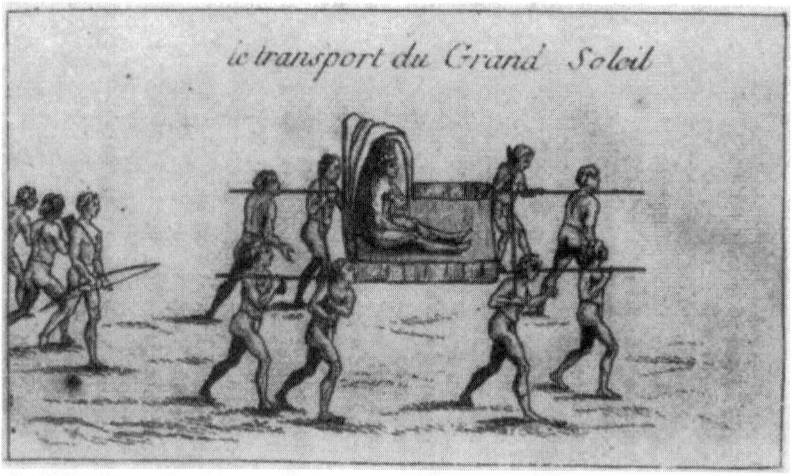

The king of the Natchez, called the Great Sun, was borne on a litter wherever he went. Stiggins, whose mother was a full-blooded Natchez, was offered the kingship by a remnant group of Natchez living in Alabama. The drawing is by Le Page Du Pratz, from Histoire de la Louisiane.
(Photograph courtesy of SMITHSONIAN INSTITUTION, BUREAU OF AMERICAN ETHNOLOGY*)*

and easily without the loss of any of their own blood. But their joy was of short duration. They equipped themselves with the spoils of their vanquished neighbors: arms, clothing, provisions, and hats, which last they particularly admired. They had no idea that there were any Frenchmen to avenge their horrid deed. In their enthusiasm to take possession of the empty garrison that they so easily obtained, they unanimously concluded and even prompted his majesty and all his suite and all who could get quarters to remove therein as the buildings were more commodious than those of the town. Then, after they had arranged their new habitation and got all snug and secure, the king sent out the usual hunting party headed by one of his nephews. But after their hunting excursion was over and they returned, behold their surprise to see a number of ships moored in front of the fort and apparently the whole of their tribe in the act of embarking under the guard and control of two rows of white men with hats on similar to those worn by the people that they destroyed. From the following circumstance I judge that the whole of the tribe were not captured as there is a people on the south waters of the Missouri who call themselves Natchez, who probably made their escape when those in the fortress were surrounded and captured. All that were shipped off by the French were insulated and settled in the island of St. Domingo where their progeny now remain.

Their arms were bows and arrows pointed with either sharpened bone or pieces of flint. With those weapons they attacked their enemy or killed their game for subsistence. When those that had been hunting returned and saw their tribe embark on the ships and disappear down the river, they could not imagine what would be the result of their destination and fate, so in their incertitude and perplexity they concluded to leave their forlorn case with the seat of their ancestors forever and in the scenes of a new and untried home forget the wreck of their tribe who they expected were doomed to slavery and wretchedness. Having had an intercourse and friendship with the Chickasaws, they made to them first, where some took up their abode, and some with the Cherokees, but the greater part headed by the royal family made a compact of assimilation with the Abekas, or Creek tribes, and settled in the Talladega Valley. They remained thus sequestered about twenty-five years when, at the instance of their chief, they all made their final exit and settled in the valley and by their compact became a member of the Ispocoga body.

This remnant of the Natchez tribe to this distant day are unfriendly to the French people. Their ancient manners and customs, it is said, were similar to those of the Abekas; so they had to make no change in their habits of life by their removal. These statements were handed down to the most ancient of the present day by their forefathers, who were spectators, though in their infancy, of what had happened to and in their tribe.

They have a belief in a supreme being but no worship or adoration. Though they generally talk about good and bad actions in their life, I never could understand that they had any idea of rewards or punishments in future, for they most generally believe in another life here or in a place they cannot describe. They keep the Busk festival in a very devout and sacred manner.[29]

Near one of their towns in the valley, not very far from Soto's fortification, there is a cavern said to be near a quarter of a mile long, dissected by many divisions. Such Indians as have been in it say that it is peopled by fairies. They had never seen any because they have the power of being imperceptible, but they had seen their tracks, and knew that they lived on the innumerable bats and swallows that stay in there. It was entered by some men many years since, a half-century ago; they found human bones in the first room and right by him carved in a rock, "I. W. Wright, 1723."[30]

In the address to my narrative I said as a prelude I would intersperse an occasional tradition. Therefore I will relate one retained by the Natchez tribe and related by them as a matter handed down through successive generations for their information. I insert it to show that in olden time their patriarch knew or heard in some way of the deluge, and the primary information or knowledge he had of it had got blended with traditional fiction. It is said that speech and rational power was given to man alone; and he by his knowledge and understanding is enabled to make the other creatures subservient to him, so that he rules and manages them in a way most conducive to his will and their comfort in life. But when the gift of speech is imparted to a dumb creature, it is to be observed as a matter of inspiration to the beast purposed by the Great Spirit to be words of sacred truth from himself through the creature.

As a manifest proof of the foregoing remarks, [it was said] that there was a large assemblage of the ancients on some particular occasion, in times of yore, when to their surprise they were accosted by a little dog, who, having gaped and yawned in a particular whining manner, began in articulate words to bemoan their sudden fate. He called on them individually to look between his ears first toward sunset and then every other direction and see their final termination of life. They looked accordingly as he said, but they could see nothing; but on a second bidding, they could see mountains of water rolling toward them. He bade them fly to the mountains for safety and to escape death. So they fled, but only a few of them reached the mountains, most being overtaken and overwhelmed by the waving torrent of water.

The "old man of sorrow" was one among them who escaped by his flight to the mountains. He is called in their tongue Tam-seal-hous-hous-opah.[31] He uttered his wailing and lamentations continually, and in tears of sorrow he mourned for all that perished, and his sorrows likewise extended to the living, whom he took under his care and tutored by good words the best way to live in future to shun the paths of destruction. The earth was overwhelmed by the billows of water and no one survived that did not attain the summit of the mountains. From these was the earth repeopled. Who this old man of lamentation or sorrow was may be a question; but as I never heard any more of him, I shall leave him as I heard of him, without any conjecture relative to him, to be solved by the inquisitive and the ancient of days.

Ispocogas

While I am in the view of relating traditions, I will insert one of the Ispocoga tribe relating to their former compact with the Shawanose. The part of the nation calling themselves Ispocogas are composed of the large and smaller towns on the Tallapoosa River to its head and those of the Chattahoochee River, excepting the Hitchitees and Uchees.

It is related that once in times past the Ispocoga and Shawanose tribes made a resolution and formed a compact by which they were thereafter to consolidate their interests; the two tribes to be but one in the future, and perform their yearly custom of thanksgiving and other rites of religious ceremony as one people. For they at that time lived bordering on each other's territory, the Shawanose in and about Savannah in the state of Georgia.[32] So in accord with their compact, they deposited with the keepers of the national square of one of the tribes their calumet tobacco pipes, bells, and war club called by them Attussa, with all of their emblems of peace and friendship together with twelve pieces of brass described as follows: six of them were oval of about eight inches long and seven inches in the widest part. The other six are about nine inches long and five in width, made square, bearing a resemblance to ancient soldier breastplates. They all belonged to the Ispocoga tribe. Three of the oval and three of the square kind made six to a set when exhibited. They are never exhibited but in their fasting and feasting to commemorate the new corn crop. So they deposited two sets of the above plates in their national square according to compact.

The united tribes of Ispocoga and Shawanose performed their ceremonies together with concord for a length of time. But through some unknown reason or occurrence which the Ispocogas attribute to the unstable and fickle disposition of the Shawanose, the Shawanose formed a resolution to secede from the union and national compact, and remove. No remonstrance of the other tribe against it could alter their determination, so they dissolved their union by emigrating northwardly. When they moved they carried off six of the sacred brass plates, three oval and three of the square kind, which the Shawanose have retained possession of ever since. They were seen by some Creeks first in the care of the old prophet at Tippacanoe, about the time he fought General Harrison; and not long since they were still in his possession over the Mississippi. The brass plates were seen by some Creek chiefs who visited that tribe, to whom they were exhibited with a traditional detail of how they came in possession of them, which account corroborated with the Ispocoga tradition of their loss.[33]

Hitchitees

The Hitchitees live on the Chattahoochee River about the mouth of Uchee Creek in a body to themselves,[34] but are considered by the other tribes as a part of the national body. In their local concerns and town meetings they use their native tongue, which is similar to the Alabama tongue, being a mongrel of the above and the Choctaw tongue.[35] They were once Seminolas of Florida.[36] The word Seminolas in the native tongue denotes a stray. Any beast that has strayed from the original flock or fold is called a Seminola. No doubt the Hitchitees from their speaking a mixed tongue were a Seminola from one of the aforementioned tribes.[37] They would number at this time about one thousand. Their chiefs take rank with the other chiefs of the nation of the same grade.

I have traced and made an exposition of national genealogy by tribes as far as information or recollection will serve me at this time. My reason for hitherto having confined my narrative only to the Upper Creeks, as they are called who live on the Coosa and Tallapoosa, without averting to their connection with the other parts of the tribe on the Chattahoochee, called the Lower Creeks, was according to a plan I had in view. First I had planned to treat of them as two independent departments, but on reflection I conceived them to be one body with two heads, who consolidate their detached and independent department for national energy and common utility. Second, it would save a tedious and prolix exposition of their local situations and environs.

Before I proceed to delineate their form of government, I must necessarily mention to the reader that, should I in the time of writing this narrative gain any further light about any of the aforesaid tribes, either of genealogy, tradition, or custom worthy of notice, I shall insert it in an afterpiece. I shall do this to avoid digression and confusion in my narrative, as much as possible, not saying that I shall keep clear of prolixity or digression; but my wish is to keep every circumstance comformably circumscribed under the proper head.

Government

The form of government under which the Creeks live is a tyrannical oligarchy in its principles, and practiced under that head to the full extent.[38] At a slight view most people suppose and say that it is a democracy on republican principles, but it is far different.

All public business, whether of a national or private character, is done by the chiefs, though the nation is summoned in what is termed their grand council, where the state of the nation is supposed to be examined and oral laws made. The assembly say not a word in the matter, for while in their sittings, the assembled body of the nation sit as mutes without being consulted in any manner. A few chiefs in the council house make the laws without condescending to ask an opinion or approbation of the national body, which is merely convened to hear what is done.

After a law is digested by the chiefs, the national convention is informed of its tendency by the orator of the nation in a very exact and precise manner. The orator informs them of all that has been transacted. When they are made acquainted with the new law, they are the most obedient subjects under the sun to the penalties of it, be it oppression or not. Should they infringe the law, they will suffer beating, confiscation of their property, or even death without a murmur or family resentment. Moreover, should an Indian be obstreperous in contending for his right of property or otherwise, or obtrude on the right or even interest of a chief, the chiefs can so far tyrannize after a consultation as to have him beaten or slain, as a common disturber of the peace without any other imputation of guilt than as a lawbreaker, as they term it.

Towns

For a better distribution of their public business such as work of planting and tending the corn, the town field, and gathering the yupon or cassene leaves for the black drink, every man of age is obliged to do his part or be fined according to his circumstance.

The inhabited part of the nation is laid out in town districts designated from some creek, ridge, or other well-known point. The boundary is organized into certain town corporated precincts under the moral guardianship of their mic-cul-ga (the plural of micco), a term of gradation more applicable to the office of overseer or guardian in my conception than to that of king (as most people will interpret it). Many towns have at least one tenth of the population for mic-cul-ga, which is none too many for guardians to watch over them and moralize their conduct, but it is far too many kings for one town or principality.

When it is thought necessary by the principal men or committee of townsmen to make a new micco, they proceed very ceremoniously to his inauguration. Without previously consulting him on the subject, at their town house assembly they advance up to him and call him in a loud, long, and shrill tone by a name that he is thereafter to go by, with the addition of Micco; for instance, Yo-ho-lo Micco, or Ispocoga Micco. At the same time they smear his face all over with white clay. . . .

Though some of the miccos rise to be principal chief, it is by merit, for the office is to admonish, regulate, and keep in peace the townspeople, who regard them with respect and deference.

There are other applicable surnames given to distinguish their town police. They attend the appointed national calls only as mutes, for in the national assembly none have a voice but such as are appointed to national purposes. Their other formalities I shall embrace in the succeeding chapters.

Chiefs

In former days, in the time of the Creeks' self-importance and undisturbed government, before an agent was located in their nation by the U.S. to improve their morals and reform their customs, their ordained chiefs[39] were more rude, active, despotic, and more frequent in their mandates of tyranny and not nearly so uniform and circumspect in their deportment as now toward the common man.

In latter years the principal chiefs or great men of the

nation have been increased to about fifteen in number. Their nomination has been approved by the agent of the government and recognized by all the tribes. They are invested with power and authority to superintend the affairs of their national government with the incumbent duties annexed, such as receiving the national salary from the agent of the U.S. and paying their public debts. They seemingly do this with a national concurrence, for they never undertake or do any important business without a national convention. After the chiefs deliberate and through their orator inform the assembled body of the nation what they have determined, they dismiss the people.

MANNERS AND CUSTOMS

Hospitality

The most prominent, and I believe the most uniform, feature in the character of the Creeks, which shows itself constantly, is their civility and innocent deportment to each other and especially to a stranger that may travel among them who is sociable and seems to conform to their customs and manners, without being self-important or asking too many impertinent questions, which will often disgust them and conclude in bad consequence. To my knowledge they are not a people to utter a remark or word to hurt the feelings of anyone, unless they are in a state of intoxication. Should they press a joke even on a friend or acquaintance so far as to be disagreeable and likely to ruffle his temper, they will immediately apologize and withhold. It rarely happens to hear one of them at any time reflect on the conduct or reputation of another. If there should be a man of general bad repute, it will be taken up and related by one of their miccos, without pointing out any person in particular. . . .

Should there be an instance of a person in the town so churlish of his eatables as to be inhospitable to one of their own people, especially to a traveling stranger, such a niggardly person is termed a nobody. Of all people they are the most tenacious of their reputation in hospitality. On the entrance of a stranger into one of their huts, he is immediately requested to sit down. As an introduction, he is asked his residence, destination, and business. Such questions are so common among them that they are replied to satisfactorily and in a brief manner. In the meanwhile the stranger is supplied with eatables; this is uniformly done at every house where he may call. Provisions bestowed to an acquaintance or stranger are put forth with a welcome which need not be doubted, should they compose the last morsel they have got. . . . To doubt his hearty welcome would unutterably hurt his feelings.

Though their custom of hospitality may be laudable and beneficial, it is both good and bad. If it is beneficial to keep the traveler and stranger from hunger and starvation, it also keeps a great many of the townspeople sauntering from door to door in loafing idleness. If no one will clothe them they are perfectly satisfied, for every house will feed them. They are in general disinterested to a degree of negligence either in the distribution of their provisions to eat or the means for the acquisition of it or wealth. They are free from the inquietude, contention, and frauds that so often produce strife and feuds among the interested and careful part of mankind.

Many years may intervene before you see two sober Indians quarrel about property. In their sober moments they seem to be totally disinterested in their own concerns; all the avenues to lucrative or other passions in them are absorbed in their wish to be social and civil to each other. It is not that their passions are indifferent either to the ease of wealth or possession of property, for they are very fond of possessing property even if they make no more use of it than the possessing of it. In consequence of their habitual idleness, all laborious pursuits tending to lucrative purposes are thought by them to be beyond their effect. Without looking forward for ways and means or even trying, they count the completion of it (if attended with the least difficulties) insurmountable, and submit it to oblivion. All their difficulties in life are caused by their inaction and want of energetic measures. I have noticed that they do not lack comprehension in any intricate piece of mechanism, having an idea of all its points and bearings to effect it; so that their genius for mechanical purposes is of no use to them, being paralyzed for the want of energetic action.

I think it necessary to contrast two topics of their life and action at this time, that is, taking into consideration their brotherly love and national attachment to each other while they are in a natural and sober state, and extremities of the opposite when in a state of intoxication, which is now a habit extending from the national chiefs to the poorest dregs of the nation. . . . Many thinking men view such scenes of intoxication with horror and pity when they consider the human depravity. Chiefs and common men and women will wallow in filth and mire so long as they can raise the means to purchase spirits to drink. During such time of frenzy they will fight each other indiscriminately, frequently taking each other's lives; and when such fracas is over they attribute the whole scene to the spirits they have drunk, very truly saying it was not them but the liquor that was in them that fought, well knowing their peaceable disposition toward each other when in their natural state of sobriety.[40] So I leave their pernicious drink.

Black Drink

I shall now enter on their uniform custom of drinking their *assee,* which is a very strong black tea used by them without any sugar, made of yupon or cassene leaves. The drink is called by the white man among them the black drink.[41] It is customary at this time and may have been for ages back for the men to meet at the town house or square in every town at least once a week. In the Tuckabatchees, the principal town, they meet every morning to drink their *assee,* which is prepared for use in the following manner at all places. It is parched first in a large pot of their own manufacture of clay, until the leaves are brown. Then water is applied to the full of the pot and boiled by a man appointed to that service. After boiling, it is cooled in large cooling pans of the same manufacture by one of the oldest chiefs of the town. When it can be poured over his finger without scalding, it is cool enough to drink. It is then put into two gourds that hold nearly a gallon, each with a hole in it of about three quarters of an inch in diameter, at which hole they suck it out. The gourds of *assee* are ceremoniously handed round the square to every man by men selected for the purpose. It is drunk as it is made, without sugar or any other embellishment.

It is a singular thing to think how this tea operates on them after they drink it. After they have drunk it they retain it in their stomachs for nearly a half-hour. They can discharge their stomachs of it as often as they drink it, with seeming ease, spouting it out of their mouths as it were by eructation, after four or five drinks and discharges of their stomachs at different times of nearly a quart at a time. It acts as a tonic. By the process their stomachs are well rinsed and braced up. The taste of the black drink is not disagreeable to the stomach, being not unlike very strong black tea and nearly of a black color. The black drink being over, the men disperse at or near ten o'clock.

No doubt their custom of drinking the black drink originated through political motives, for the purpose of assembling the townspeople frequently at the town house or square in order to keep them united.

The harmony among the people of a town seems to be cemented by an affection as strong toward each other as the sons of Jacob of old in their association. The usages and customs of every town are similar, and men all know the unity and sympathy of a townspeople. The men of one town will approach another town with seeming diffidence though the towns may be contiguously situated. As such is their practice in their more enlightened time, their approaches toward each other's towns and toward strangers must have been with extreme timidity and caution in their natural and savage state.

And as they seldom change their town site, it is probable they are situated as they were at the time of Ferdinand Soto's visit more than three centuries ago.[42]

Ceremonial Pipe Smoking

I have observed among them another trait of national character: in the public meetings whether for black drink or national council, the Indians appear studiously to wish to show an importance in themselves and independence of character. They will perceptibly assume a grave, sedate, consequential deportment, especially their chiefs and head men. They appear for a while to a bystander to be careless of all nature and each other. At length nature seems to predominate and they show their true disposition. When they commence smoking their pipe, the spell seems to be removed. After a few draws of smoke from their pipe, they cordially hand it to the next at hand who may make use of the contents of the pipe or pass it to the next man. A constant repetition of such civilities engenders a familiarity in the community at large that would not have taken place otherwise, as they seldom have any interesting conversation to impart or attend to.

With a stranger it is customary with them to use hesitation, even should they wish to converse with him. They accost each other with studied and manifest civility, to which they reciprocally receive an answer equally ceremonious until an acquaintance takes place.

They in a general way appreciate a good character very little either in themselves or anyone else in the common scenes of life. There is no perceptible difference made by them between a discreet, virtuous woman and one of ill fame and lewd practices. In the common standing of society, it will equally extend to men. Thieves, murderers, and other evil practitioners are not held in disrepute, nor are they subject to either scorn or reproach. They very often make head men or miccos of such men, so that their actions are in unison with their natural inclinations and only amenable to their customary laws. So far they are irreproachable and true sons of nature and inclination.[43]

Marriage and Widowhood

It is customary among the Creeks when a man selects the one that he wants for his wife, he goes to some of her relatives, frequently without speaking to her or consulting her, to open the subject of his wishes for an alliance. (Or he has it done by some of his kinspeople.) Most properly he goes to the uncle of the woman on the mother's side, who has entire control of his nieces in cases of marriage or otherwise. Should the offer meet his approbation, he does not protract his consent or disavowal longer than he can lay the proposal before her relations of the mother's side, who are counted her actual kinsmen and women. In this assembly the candidate's disposition and other qualities are discussed. Neither the father or anyone in the woman's father's family are ever consulted in case of marriage of his children, as he and they are not of the same family. The primogenitureship of all families descends from the mother. The above I will explain hereafter.

When the uncle or relation has informed the rest of his kindred or clansmen of the proposal of marriage and by whom made, they seldom refuse their assent. There is no fuss made of fortune portion or chattels on either side, after such consultation. If the suitor should visit their dwelling before they do him, he is informed of the family acquiescence. The bridal bed is publicly made for the pair to make a conclusion of the courtship and marriage. After the consummation of the marriage and he finds her in clothes, should she be the first wife formally married to him and passes the Boos-ke-tah[44] with him, she is received as his actual wife by his kinsfolk and all others.

After the solemnization of the new corn feast passes over them, she is bound to him during life or his pleasure; that is, should she be indolent and given to quarrel with him and inattentive to his wants and disobedient to his commands in any of the aforesaid cases, he can make complaint to her family of such, and quit her, and marry another without a murmur of her clan or family.

In case she should prove a lewd woman and inconstant to him, she can be punished by his family or clanspeople; they beat her with large sticks until she cannot move and then cut off both her ears close to the head. The punishment may be inflicted contrary to the will or consent of her husband, which frequently happens. After her punishment, her husband may repudiate her or retain her still as his wife.

As polygamy is permitted only by the wife's consent, the men use a great deal of force and craft to obtain it. In order to keep clear of the crime of adultery, all a man's after-married wives have to stay at their homes, unless his first wife lets one stay with her in the house and do all the drudgery of the place as a maid. By his wife's consent a man can take as many wives or concubines as he chooses to maintain. Should his wife disapprove of his having a concubine and he obtain one against her will, his wife's relations or clanspeople have it in their power to beat him and his concubine or second wife with sticks and cut off their ears. Afterward he is separated from his wife and has to retain the one beaten on his account. Nevertheless he has it in his power to keep the old wife single for four years or four Boos-ke-tahs, unless she elopes with a man and eludes the vigilance of his clan to the ensuing Boos-ke-tah. Then she is ever after clear of punishment for her adultery. She is finally separated from her first husband and the control of his clanswomen. It is customary for the clanspeople not to tolerate the widowed man to play *loke* or [ ] a woman,[45] nor a woman a man, during their separation.

I have gone through their marriage ceremonies and touched on their state of widowhood. I think it necessary to enlarge and be more explicit on the subject. On the death of either married partner, the survivor is made a widow in the following manner: should the woman be the survivor, immediately after the man's burial, the women on his mother's side, or his clanswomen, who are all the widow's guardians or retainers, proceed to divest her of her gay apparel and her other ornaments of dress such as brooches, beads, and necklaces, and loose her hair and spread it over her shoulders. In this situation she is to remain and mourns four years for her deceased husband, unless she is sooner relieved by the compassion of her retainers. At any time of her widowhood one of her deceased husband's brothers or cousins on his mother's side can relieve her by taking her to wife himself. Should he have a wife at the time, it cannot be murmured at by anyone, as he is in duty naturally bound to raise seed to his brothers. . . . Should the clanswomen think her in a bad situation, they very often before the expiration of her widowhood have compasssion on her forlorn state and give her a comb to comb her hair, or some of them comb her hair for her, and invest her with such clothes and ornaments as those she had before her widowhood. After they have gone through this ceremony, she is at liberty to marry whom she pleases. But should she not await the formal relief of her retainers, but in contempt of their prerogative take to combing her hair or marrying a husband, they can treat her as in any other case of adultery should she do it before the expiration of four years or four Boos-ke-tahs from the death of her husband. But if she marries a man and elopes with him and eludes the vigilance of her retainers to the expiration of the ensuing anniversary of the new corn crop, then she is free of their constraint and can live with her husband without fear of punishment. Her husband . . . is inseparably bound to her; he cannot be implicated in the crime of adultery with her, all the crime being imputed to her lewd disposition and incontinency. The same constraint, ceremony, and restriction are observed with the man, should his wife die first.[46]

Corn Festival

I have made frequent mention of the celebration of the anniversary of the new corn crop, called by the Creeks Boos-ke-tah, "sacred purifying," which is the only time I ever saw them act as though they paid adoration to the All-Supreme. When they are preparing to go to the festival they seem to solemnize their mind and actions as a devout person does entering a church to worship.

It is evident that originally the Boos-ke-tah must have had great weight in the Creeks' political movements, for after its celebration proceedings are stopped against any offender where life and death is not concerned; stealing is not exempted. All other misdemeanors pass into oblivion and a new score is begun for the ensuing festival.

The Coosawdas hold a festival more than the rest of the

nation. They annually celebrate the coming of the new crop of beans with the same ceremonies as they do the corn. . . . When the head men of a town see the public corn is full in the ear and fit for use, they set a day and inform the townspeople when the sacred festival is to commence. Before the day arrives, they nominate some of their *emathlas*[47] ("gone at his bidding") to boil their physic that they drink and wash with, to purify themselves. Of their most respectable chiefs they nominate three to officiate in the duties of sacred priests or doctor. They then send some of the *emathlas* to gather a bush that acts as a quick and powerful emetic. They call it *micco ho-you-ejah*.[48] It is a "chief's cathartic." They break enough to last the festival out. The bush in appearance is very much like the low myrtle bush, but it bears no berries.

When the festival day arrives, all the townspeople put out their fires and repair to their town house or square where they commence the sacred festival. They have particular songs and dances for it. They dance during the festival at intervals. Their singers are generally men of eminence, invited as proficient singers of other towns, and they take it as a mark of distinction to receive an invitation for that purpose. After all have congregated, the select men boil physic, and those nominated to officiate as sacred men make a fire out of the public way so that they may not be polluted by the touch of unpurified persons during their strict penance, as they consider their persons sacred during this office.

They proceed to boil their *awo-teach-caw*, which is an emetic.[49] After it is thoroughly boiled, the three men selected for the sacred office take it, after it is put into large cooling pans of clay, and prepare it for drinking and washing with. Each man takes a pan and sets it before him and commences the process of cooling, having his head covered and a joint of cane in his hand. They each sing a song of requests and thanks in a low voice to the Giver or Taker of Breath, called E-saw-ga-misse.[50] At intervals the singer sticks his cane joint into the pan of *awo-teach-caw* and blows the virtue of the song of requests into the pan of physic in a solemn manner, so that it might operate for good to them that drink thereof. It is a quick and rapid emetic and drunk for that purpose by all the men; the women wash their children with it.

The Creek Indians have no variation in their annual celebration of the new crop of corn, having particular songs and dances for the festive purpose. The commemoration in every town lasts two days, except for the minor villages where it lasts twenty-four hours. The Tuckabatchee town, being the metropolis of the nation, has a variety of ways to celebrate their solemn feast. They hold it six days. It is attended always by a large congregation who resort there to see and be seen.

In their six days of Boos-ke-tah, neither those set apart as doctors of physic, nor those appointed to show the strict rules or penance necessary on the occasion, eat or drink anything but the consecrated emetic, which they take profusely every day of the festival. They neither speak to nor touch a woman during the time, as such procedure would inevitably ruin their thanksgiving song and incur destruction not only to him that does it but to the community at large. Nor will they shake hands with or touch an unpurified friend during the time of their officiating.

The whole festival is conducted with a grave, superstitious solemnity to the last day. On the last day they take out and exhibit the aforementioned six brass or breastplates. The plates are carried around by three men, one in each hand, in the day's dances. After their exhibition in the dances the plates are laid in their depository under the seats that hold the mats on which the chiefs sit in the council square. The plates are kept under the constant care of two men.

It is said that three of the brass plates have signs of hieroglyphics on them, while others say they can trace Hebrew characters in a circle in the central part of the three oval ones. As they are scoured and burnished every year before they are exhibited, no doubt the characters are nearly defaced. The traditional account of how the Creeks came by the plates is that they were thrown or handed down by the Giver or Taker of Breath, E-saw-ga-missee, with an assurance that, so long as they used them undefiled in their festivals, no people could divest them of their festival ceremonies or country.

On the same day they exhibit their manner of attack in warfare. Several effigies are placed about in the square to be attacked in a hostile manner by men appointed for the purpose. To show their skill in coming on their enemy by stealth, they come on the effigies with all imaginable caution, as though unperceived by them as an enemy. When they get near the square they raise the war scream and charge the effigies, shoot, tomahawk, and scalp them. Though pursued by others, they make their escape as they would in an actual attack.

As many have passed their time fasting, it is necessary

to eat of the new corn. As all things in their political life have a new beginning, it is necessary to have a new fire to cook their corn and other eatables. That morning four men are appointed to that duty. They each take a block with a small incision in it and a round stick; they apply the stick in the indention of the block and roll it in the palm of the hand until it takes fire by the friction. There is great joy when the new fire is made. Every family in the town, and adjacent townspeople, take the new fire home to cook with for that year.

In the process of the festival, the young men are divested of their given names from infancy and invested with war names. By his war name a man is known the rest of his life. It is done thus: it is intimated to the young man by one of the chiefs or warriors (for either can give names) the name he is thereafter to assume. When the time arrives for the ceremony, one of the chiefs or warriors rises from his seat and calls the name in a shrill, long tone of voice. At the call, the young man rises and picks up the war club or mallet, called by them *attussa*, and goes to the chief or warrior, who informs him that he is now named as other men and can now assume the manners and customs of other men. He puts a feather in his head. When that is done, the newly dubbed man raises his war club above his head, starts a long whoop, and runs around in a circle to where he started; when he stops he cries, "Youh-youh." From that time he is a man with a name.

Clans

The strongest link in Creek political and social standing is their clanship or families. By their observance of clans they are so united that no part of the nation is detached from the other. All are linked harmoniously and consolidated as one large, connected family. By their family-prescribed rules there is no part of the nation but a man can find his clansmen or family connection.

The nation consists of nine clans or families: Wind, Bear, Panther, Bird, Polecat, Fox, Potato, Red Paint, and Isfauna, which is composed of many small ones.[51] Of all the clans the largest and most privileged is the Wind family.[52] They exclusively are permitted to rise with their sticks and punish their own clanspeople three times to take satisfaction of an offender toward one of their family, for minor offenses such as committing adultery or stealing. Should any of the other clans rise with their sticks and punish once and the offender escape, they must lay down their sticks and punish no more. The Boos-ke-tah is a curb and restraint to the privilege of the Wind family, for if an offender escapes after one of the Wind family has punished him, and he keeps out of their reach until the celebration of the Boos-ke-tah, they are obliged to withhold punishment.

All the clans in the nation take their family descent from the mother, being of the same family of the mother; they can only take a part with that family. The father and his clan or family are only the father's family to the children, as he and his clan or family have no legal say or interest in the children's family concerns. All the men of their father's clan or family are called their father. The women are generally called their grandmother. The men of the mother's family older than themselves are their uncles, being their mother's brothers. All of their own age or younger are called their brother, and the old women of their mother's clan are called grandmother or aunt. Grown women of the Wind family are to be called grandmother by the other families. All the clans are connected as friends or some distant relation through the nation.

The clan is the strong link of the Creeks' political existence, a complete curb and cement to their ferocious and vindictive nature when irritated, although their implacable and revengeful passion cannot be mitigated by the interference of clan or family when one of another clan, even if by chance, should kill one of their blood relations on the mother's side. Their customary law in this is similar to the law of the Jewish legislation in reference to the manslayer, excepting the city of refuge, for their law is literally, "who so sheddeth man's blood his blood must be shed."[53]

Time and distance cannot palliate the clan's revenge, for should the perpetrator make his escape, one of his brothers or cousins on his mother's side is taken. One of his blood kindred or himself must atone for the one lost, male for male, female for female. Even accidents are frequently made a matter of atonement. For instance, if one is on business for another person and killed by his horse, the employer or one of his brothers or cousins must atone with his life for the death, because, they say, had it not been for him and his business, the death would not have happened. Such reasoning may seem strange when expressed by a people possessing predestinarian principles. When they reflect on any bad accident or misfortune happening to them, it is a solace and comfort to them that it was unavoidable, as it was foreordained that such and such a thing was to be.

I will narrate a circumstance of a deplorable nature that

happened to the Singer, who at that time was head chief of the Creek nation. I bring it forward to show the Creeks' true character in regard to retaliation for the loss of one of their blood kindred, though their own principal chief was the victim of their national custom.

About the year 1808 the Singer covertly agreed with Colonel Hawkins, the U.S. Indian agent, that he would go under pretense of hunting to explore the country on both sides of the Mississippi River. If he found a country that would suit the nation, he would exert his influence with the nation to sell their place of nativity by treaty and remove the nation to the new country.

Without letting his brothers, who accompanied him on the hunting excursion, know his designs, the Singer struck the Mississippi high up and crossed over to the west side. They had been over there but a short time when they came on the camps of part of a tribe that were their mortal enemies. They soon made an attack on one of the camps, and in the conflict the Singer lost one of his brothers. After the encounter with the Husaws, they returned to the east side, thinking it not safe to remain. There has ever been interminable warfare among the original tribes residing on the east and west sides of the Mississippi River. With extreme and guarded caution they approached each other's haunts. Their trade and intercourse with the white people resulted in similar stuff for clothing and similar fashion of their dress, and it was hardly possible for them to recognize one of their own tribe from another without a salutation. So it happened in this case. As one of the Singer's brothers was on his researches near the Mississippi River, he saw an Indian crossing his way, and supposing him to be an enemy who had crossed the river for mischief, shot him dead. On approaching to get his scalp, he recognized him to be a Cusseta town man, one of his own nation. He returned to the camp and informed his brothers that he had unluckily killed a man of their own nation through a mistaken idea that he was a Wa-sas-sa (so they call all their enemies on the west of the Mississippi).[54] When their man did not return to the camp at night, the people of the Cusseta camp concluded that some accident had befallen him, and they went in search for him the next day. In their researches they came on the Singer who was alone in the camp. He proceeded to recount to them the nature of the sad affair and that it happened by a mistake of his brother who supposed the man to be a Wa-sas-sa who had crossed the river for mischief. . . . The Cussetas appeared satisfied with his account and convinced that it happened through a mistake. The Singer informed them that his brother and camp people were gone in search of their camp to inform the Cussetas of the particulars of the accident. After they had eaten with him they started back for their camp. On their way they concluded that, as their brother was slain and it was acknowledged by whom, and as the slayer who had wantonly spilled their brother's blood was out of the way, it would be only right to retaliate for the deed by depriving him of his brothers by the same means. So they returned to the camp and killed the Singer for his brother's killing theirs. . . .

If the Singer, after his examination of the new country, had lived to return, his representations of its superiority to their place of nativity may have awakened a sense of emigration in the nation even at that distant period; but his death will leave that matter ever in doubt.

CREEK-WHITE POLITICS

British Agents

In narrating such part of Creek history as I have attained, I shall merely narrate the circumstance and not attempt to be exact as to time in a chronological order, but make it a rule to be as concise in a miscellaneous manner as I can, and move on the road of truth in my telling. I have obtained information with as much perspicuity and precision as the nature of the case will admit. I shall adduce only such information as recollection and oral testimony can furnish.

I shall begin a commencement of the Creeks' political career as far back as the American Revolution. They took a decided part with Britain through the persuasion of influential men among them when they were neutral. They were easily buoyed up through friendship with the English for their kind and friendly treatment to them without regarding or knowing the cause of contest between the British and the colonies. I may further say that they were under the influence of the English agent among them, who was sent especially from Scotland to strengthen their attachment toward England.[55] He was not negligent toward his destination at the momentous crisis but made use of his influence to irritate them against the United States. In his endeavors and false representations he was assisted by the Scottish traders who resided in the nation. Many of them were connected by interest and otherwise to Tate.[56] When the traders saw how wholly he was devoted to the cause he advocated, they, in order to make their court to him with ease, and please themselves, had frequent English peace talks for the Indians. The traders inflamed their passion against the United States by their falsities until they made the Indians determine on action. The Creeks are naturally warlike and easily persuaded to mischief or warlike enterprises. So as was expected, the deluded Indians advocated the British cause in word and action, instead of keeping a neutral station as policy and interest would wisely dictate to them.

In their frenzy the Creeks immediately submitted themselves to be led by John Galphin, James Leslie, and Charles Weatherford[57] to assist the British, who were besieged in Savannah and Augusta in repelling the assailants. At both the above sieges, no man evidenced more activity and courage than the ruling chief of the nation called Mortar, who resided in the Hillabee town.[58] In a night encounter with General Wayne's division, on a trip down to try a relief of one of the sieges, he was severely wounded. On the first attack the Indians charged the lines so quickly that they successfully entered the American camp and put to rout the part of the infantry or guard who opposed their way, but who only retreated to the main body of the camp to reinforce. In the meantime, the Indians, supposing that they had won an entire victory, fell to plundering the camp. They fell over a puncheon of old rum. As it ever has been and is now an established maxim with them to believe in the wonder workings and cheerful glee of the delicious stimulant, in their enthusiasm they concluded that as they had taken the camp and achieved an easy victory over the soldiers, even taking their rum, that they had the right (when aided by a craving disposition) to drink it up. But their easy victory proved a mistake, for General Wayne was not so easily to be vanquished. He came on them with his division of veterans about the time that they had got their minds absorbed in rum, unwary and careless of an enemy or anything else, to the degree that they had unguardedly divested themselves of their weapons. In this situation, though surprised with the point of the bayonet, they attempted to maintain an unequal contest against double their number, which of course they could not do. After standing the point of the bayonet a short while, the Indians broke through the enemy and pursued their way to their friends as they first intended.[59]

It is notorious that all Creek Indians who have had any intercourse or transaction with the British or their emissaries were ever partial to them and favorable to their interest. Many an old man of the present day expatiates on the candid, honest, and liberal disinterestedness of the British as friends to the Indians in their talks and in their dealings. They seemingly remark with wrath the contrast between the British and the Americans: that in their contracts with the Indians the English dealt with equitable candor and justice, but with deceit and self-interested political views the Americans made liberal promises to attain their purpose and only performed such part of their contracts as would suit their convenience and evidenced thereby a faint recollection of the circumstances that were material to the cause.

McGillivray Visits President Washington

From the above stated opinion of the American character, the general disposition of the Creek tribe was rancorous and undoubtedly very unfavorable to the United States from the close of the Revolutionary War to about 1794. In that year President Washington very humanely requested General McGillivray, a part Indian who was equally friendly to both parties, to take a number of influential chiefs of the nation to the seat of government, then in the city of Philadelphia,[60] which he accordingly did.

The kind reception that was given the party by the President and Cabinet was flattering, the Indians being unused to the like from white people. The paternal kindness and concern that was expressed for their welfare by the President made them reverence in his person their amiable great father and well-wisher. His clemency displayed toward them caused them to return to their home effectually reconciled to the U.S. They related with exaggerated eulogy on their return how they had been received with kindness and hospitality and entertained by their great father Washington, and how he had instructed and admonished them to pursue the way of peace and amity with all the Indian tribes, and more especially with the U.S. in whose limits they resided. As neighbors they were mutually bound to blend their interests and to cultivate a lasting friendship. For as both lived on one continent, detached by the ocean from the feuds and interests of the powers of Europe, they said they could see and understand the propriety of his reasoning. On their return home, in their grand national council, the chiefs gave a detailed account of the talks and interviews with the great beloved man.[61] . . . They were confident of the benefits that would ultimately result from the Creek nation's adopting and steadfastly pursuing said pacific principles.

Many still adhered to the wise and salutary advice of their great and adored father Washington, when Tecumseh, the earthquake, and the Spaniards, all in succession, like Pandora's box, made them waver. The first, Tecumseh, alarmed them with the expectation of some dreadful event by a repetition of his prophetic problems. The second filled them with awful expectations by its being unprecedented and unaccountable. . . . The Spaniards caused such a distraction of the nation as to make the majority without thought or hesitation enter into the ruthless war in 1813, not only among themselves but against the U.S. This war eventually nearly exterminated their nation and circumscribed their once extensive country to the late ceded limits.[62]

In accord with the President's advice, the chiefs on their return home exerted their aid and influence in assisting Captain John Chisholm, who had humanely undertaken to reconcile a war between the Creeks and the Chickasaw tribe, pending for nearly a year. The Creek tribe had commenced hostilities on some frivolous ground of misunderstanding.

The Creek Way of Making War

The Creeks wage war thus. The national council is convened, and the nature of the offence is examined in a council of high chiefs and warriors. If they conclude that the cause of collision is of so glaring a nature as to admit of no compromise or palliation of nothing but the blood of the enemy, it is a positive declaration of war.

The final conclusion of the chiefs is announced to the assembled body of the chiefs and warriors by the orator, explaining to them and the assembly the reasons why they are justified in a declaration of war.

Before they make a descent on their enemy, on a day appointed they assemble at their town house square in complete armor, all stripped and painted red, black, and white as they go into action, with their guns on their shoulders, their knives and tomahawks hanging to their sides and war clubs stuck in their belts. (A war club is shaped like a small gun about two feet long. At the curve near where the lock would be is a three-square piece of iron or steel with a sharp edge driven in, to leave a projection of about two inches.) They all take their seats as they assemble. The man who is honored to be the town leader rises and takes his stand in the square. When he raises the sacred war whoop and begins to sing and dance in the circle, the rest rise and raise the same whoop and drop in behind one another. In a very little time their singing and dancing is drowned by whooping and by firing of guns. At an appointed rendezvous on their way to the enemy, they hold another war dance in the same way as described above.

I will try to return to the former subject. After they declare war and before they commence hostilities, they gather every man, woman, and child belonging to the nation to their respective town and relatives, whether far or near. After they have collected all their kindred, they are ready to commence hostilities on the enemy. If one of the other nation is seen by them he is destroyed.

Their petty wars are wars of extermination. They are not man against man, but tribe against tribe. It is a praiseworthy action for a man or a party to kill the women and children of their enemy, more so than to kill a man who is frequently in the forest. To kill a woman shows that he was not afraid to go into enemy country, but achieved the manly deed in the enemy's very house door and escaped.

The high opinion the Creeks had of themselves gave them incentive to war on other nations. In their wish to convince the Chickasaws of their self-importance, in the summer of 1793 they made an irruption into the Chickasaw country with a collected force of nearly a thousand warriors. The warriors were headed by different chiefs, but the whole group was under the guidance of Mad Dog of Tuckabatchee (Efan Hadjo)[63] and Tobe of Talladega, a man of a desperate character and ill repute. With them as counselor was James Leslie, an old Scotch trader, who had led them near the close of the Revolution in assisting the besieged in Savannah.

The Creeks used such precaution and dispatch in their descent on their enemy that it was not known that an invasion of Chickasaw country was intended until the firing announced their arrival. They made straight for a fortress built by William Colbert and his brothers for the safety of their families and dependents. The Creeks made an assault on the fortress, which they could have taken had they made a determined attack. But they commenced their firing and frightful yelling at a considerable distance from the fort. The Chickasaws in the neighborhood, hearing the report of the guns, mounted their horses and made for the fort; but by mistake they made their way into the Creek forces, and five of them were instantly killed. The rest made their way safely into the fort. Thereafter the Creeks . . . quit their attack of the fort with precipitation and fled for their lives. Their flight was so intense and their panic so great that all entreaty was unavailing. Leslie and many of their mounted chiefs gained their front and used commands and expostulations to stop and rally them to a fight. But all was to no purpose. The Creek warriors kept on running though they outnumbered their pursuers by fifty to one. In their flight woe to the hindmost, for their pursuers for many miles selected and killed the most convenient of them without resistance. The Creeks' panic caused their overthrow.

When the Creeks made their attack on Colbert's fort it was tenanted only by seven men and their families, besides a few Negroes. With the addition of those who broke through the Creek force at the commencement of the attack, there was an aggregate number of seventeen men in all and a few Negroes who vanquished the Creek armament of nearly a thousand warriors, killing and wounding nearly a hundred of them. This defeat terminated the active operations of their war with the Chickasaws and served greatly to humble the pride of the Ispocogas. Shortly after the encounter, Captain J. Chisholm, with the assistance of others, and the chiefs of the tribes mediated a pacific treaty [with the Chickasaws], which has been unalterable ever since.

About the same time, the Creeks carried on a marauding and predatory warfare with the new settlers of Cumberland River in Tennessee who, the Indians alleged, were trespassing on their ground. The settlers had opened and were inhabiting plantations in the Creeks' principal hunting ground, which had been given to them in the partition of hunting grounds with other tribes. It was their opinion that they had the right to retain that portion of the forest unsullied and undefiled by the touch of axe or plow. They thought that so long as the forests were uncultivated they had the right to kill the game therein. What they got from the sale and barter of the skins, they used to clothe themselves and their families and get their winter supply of meat. If the land was settled by the white people and plantations opened on it, they would be in want of such supplies.

At that time the Creeks' place of trade and barter centered in Pensacola, a small Spanish town in Florida where there was established a large commercial house under the firm of Panton, Leslie, & Company, who engrossed the entire trade of the adjacent national tribes by bartering groceries and goods for their peltry and furs. White traders in the nation misadvised the Indians; by false representations they stirred them up to make reprisals for supposed injuries. They induced them eventually to commit murders among the recent settlers of Tennessee and to steal their horses, under the impressed idea that such a procedure would deter the white people from moving into the country and thereby the Creeks could do their hunting undisturbed. The dishonest traders would then buy the stolen horses from the Indians for four or five gallons of rum. They would use the horses to pack their peltry and hides to take to market. After the fur and peltry trade stopped in Europe, the packing of horses to market was of no further use. But the stealing of horses was such a habit with the white man and the red man that it continued until 1813.

The Indians by nature, even at this day, are honest though indolent and negligent to a blamable degree. They apologize for their habitual defects by asserting that before their innate passions and morals were corrupted by the white men residing among them, stealing from each other was unknown to them. Being raised poor and habituated to that life, they felt no anxiety for the goods or property of others, so they were not excited to perpetrate acts of thievery for things they did not crave or know the want of.

It is unfortunate for them that their first visitors were a debauched, indolent, dishonest set, without the fear of man or God and only afraid of labor. Had they been visited by a pious, industrious, virtuous set of men, and they permitted these men to locate among them and inculcate examples and instructions of piety, labor, and virtuous pursuits, the Indians' case at this day would have been far different. It would have saved a great effusion of innocent blood. Many a father would not have lamented the children swept from under his care by shocking circumstances. . . .

It is remarkable that the Creeks, in all the trials and meanderings of their political life, have had a magnetic predilection for the British. They would declare without reserve their adherence to them as friends, and as unreservedly express their abhorrence of the Virginians, as they term the Americans.[64] At this or any other period when they had intercourse with the British, their partiality would manifest itself by some frenzied movement, so great is their need to incur English favor.

The last notable effort the Creeks made in the American Revolution to serve their friends the British was near the close of the war. They attempted to succor their British and Tory friends besieged in Mobile by Don Galvez and the Choctaws. The Creeks raised and armed about two hundred warriors in order to raise the siege. They repaired to the place of contest headed by the Old Mortar of the Hillabee town. They went down on the east side of the Alabama River under the guidance of Richard T. Coleman, a Georgian by birth, until they reached a bluff immediately above the town of Blakely east of Mobile. There they camped, expecting to be immediately transported by their friends at Fort Charlotte to Mobile.[65] They did not know that the Spaniards and Choctaws knew their purpose. A Choctaw force with a few Spaniards crossed the bay and with about an equal force surprised the Creeks. The Old Mortar and his men, though taken unaware, were not daunted, but returned the war whoop and met their assailants with manly courage and worsted them in the onset. But the Choctaws turned the scale by an act of desperation, which is common to them when hard run in battle. They threw away their firearms and attacked with their tomahawks and scalping knives. The Ispocogas, unused to so close a combat, gave ground in all quarters, and left their leader with a few others in an unequal contest which could not last long, as many of them were wounded. The Ispocogas lost about fifty warriors, and of their wounded only a few escaped. They mostly graced the scalp pole of the Choctaws.

The Old Mortar made his escape, though mortally wounded. He died for his British friends the next day on the road about five miles above the last battleground. This was the Creeks' last scene of warfare in the American Revolution.[66]

Benjamin Hawkins

After the close of the American Revolution the Creeks still lived under the control of their own nation until about the year 1798, when the United States Government located an agent among them. Their first agent was Colonel Benjamin Hawkins.[67] From Indian eulogy he was a gentleman qualified by reputation and rectitude to fill the trust imposed on him.

In their first transactions with Hawkins the Indians distrusted him and his office. They held frequent debates among themselves on the propriety of the idea of killing him. They thought he was merely imposed on them by the Government as a spy and a snare to shackle their liberties. But in their meetings and consultations with him in an official way, they could not but admire his firm, honest, and candid deportment. The more they became acquainted with him the more they were reconciled to his office among them. They loved him for his virtuous and disinterested greatness of mind, for he expressed to them his hopes and wishes for their welfare. He took pains to learn their language, in which he was fluent in a little time. He tamed the wild savage, and by personal example and instruction he made a farmer and a husbandman of him. He taught and familiarized the Indian to the sound of the blacksmith's anvil and the weaver's baton. When he

Benjamin Hawkins, U.S. agent to the Creeks, 1797-1816. (Photograph courtesy of ALABAMA DEPARTMENT OF ARCHIVES AND HISTORY*)*

was first located among them, there did not exist in the whole nation a half-dozen fences made of rails. Indian fencing consisted of forks about two feet high and cross-staked, and poles laid in the crosses to the height they intended the fence to be. By noticing his farm and plantation as an example, many of the Creeks soon fenced with rails and enlarged their farms. Not two of them in fifty had seen the process of spinning and weaving. But by instruction, example, and encouragement Hawkins so improved the Creeks in domestic pursuits of life that by the time of the War of 1813 they were far more edified in domestic arts, industry, and civilization than at this day.

It is to be regretted that Hawkins did not live to see them enjoy the result of his progressive improvement among them. It is as lamentable that his virtuous, high, and disinterested mind did not reside within the body of his successors. The principal aim of his successors has been to devise ways to withhold from the Indians much of their stipend, without condescending to instruct the poor, untaught wretches in sober habits or domestic pursuits of life. Colonel Hawkins by his unwearied exertions and moral precepts somewhat smoothed the rough nature of men of the forest. His successors, by designed neglect, did not give wanted good counsel to induce the Creeks to pursue the path of rectitude and occupy their minds beneficially. Time has seen them slide down to the lowest verge of degradation, to become a set of consummate sots—a circumstance much lamented by the few thinking and sober tribesmen.

After they made sure that Colonel Hawkins's counsel was intended for their individual and national benefit, the chiefs gradually placed their confidence in him. They counted their national affairs safe under his management until about the year 1812, when their confidence was put to the test.

TECUMSEH AND THE AGE OF PROPHETS

The Shawnee Prophet

Two or three Coosawdas previous to 1813 accompanied some Seminolas of the Shawanose tribe to see their progenitors on the Waubash. About this time the Shawanose prophet began to propagate a belief among the northern tribes of his wonder-workings and inspired knowledge of future events.[68] The Coosawdas protracted their visit in that country long enough to absorb the prophet's notions of the white man's oppressive and domineering encroachments on Indian rights. They returned home with different opinions than those they went with.

The Shawanose prophet had convinced them of the overbearing wrongs they had suffered and of the successful revenge the Indians would have in exterminating the white people for dispossessing them wantonly and insatiably of their lands contrary to the order purposed by the Creator. In his wrath the Creator would assist the

Indians in the recovery of their lands, which he had made on purpose for their special use. He suited it for them in fruits of all kinds, acorn trees, spontaneously bearing eatables for their subsistence and comfort. Such lectures the Shawanose avowed in a prophetic manner.

The principal of the Coosawdas was Taskeegee Tustonuggee, or Ho-co-lee, which is "two" in their tongue. On their way home the Indians, under the influence of the prophet, committed outrageous murders on some unoffending families in Tennessee, for no other provocation than being white—[the whites being] a people doomed in a short time for Indian destruction, according to the prophet's prediction of the will of the Great Maker of all things.[69] At the time of the Grand Creek National Council the murderers divulged what they had done, giving themselves great merit for the act, it being according to the pleasure of God. At the same time the case was brought before the national council by the agent of the United States for satisfaction. Ho-co-lee and the others concerned in the murders were convicted of the crime by the grand national council on the evidence of their own report, and they were slain on the spot.

At this time the whole nation began to be frenzied and looked daily in expectation of a phenomenon or event of a direful nature. Rife in fanatical frenzy, they accepted Tecumseh's mad notions that he avowed to them in his public speech to the assembled body of the nation on his visit to them.[70] What heightened their astonishment into almost a certainty was a coincidence of Tecumseh's ominous remark in his speech to the shock of the earthquake and the appearance of the comet previously.[71] Two such uncommon occurrences in succession occasioned the fabrication of the most dreadful tales. Flying tales multiplied daily and were exaggerated in parts of the nation, told and received as truth. All the foolish tales had no father, for they were said to be told by first one and then another, and nobody could ascertain who. The people received as truth all Tecumseh's fanatical tales. His visit came long enough before the national council to enable him to inform them of his views on the pending conflict with the Americans and predisposed the Creeks in his favor.

During Tecumseh's stay he tried all the rhetoric he was master of to induce the Big Warrior, head of the national chiefs and the subordinate chiefs, to join in his plan for an Indian league. The plan was for all the Indian tribes on the continent to hold their lands in one common stock; the sale of any of their lands would be valid only by consent of all the tribes.

On Tecumseh's arrival the Big Warrior and Captain Isaacs listened to his peace talk,[72] accepted the calumet and tobacco, and smoked friendship with him. They learned his new war songs and dances, which were sung and danced in all the towns on the Tallapoosa before the grand national council was convened. But it was not generally known that Captain Isaacs had gone the preceding summer to Mobile and bought fifty bags of powder. Very few were in on the secret, and those who knew it were so minded in principle and inclination.

Tecumseh had said to many in private, and to the national council, that he was determined to war with the Americans. He stated the great supernatural powers he possessed. He said if he was to beat the white people they would know it by the following sign: he would ascend to the top of a mountain about four moons from that time and there he would whoop three unbounded loud whoops, slap his hands together three times, and raise his foot and stamp it on the earth three times. By these actions he could make the whole earth tremble, which would be a sign of his success in the undertaking. If such did not happen, they would know that he was to fail in the enterprise. This and many more speeches of a miraculous nature that he made did not lessen his reputation but exalted him in the estimation of the majority of the nation. They looked on him as superior and as one of the most consummate and fearless warriors of his time and a man worthy of imitation.

When Colonel Hawkins attended the Creek Grand National Council he expressed his surprise to see them so weak-minded as to be led astray and to attempt desperate measures that endangered their safety. The words of reason flowing from their beloved man did not find them all like Festus of old, deaf to the words of truth and soberness. In the Big Warrior they found a light of returning reason. Big Warrior acknowledged his and their folly; he said that he saw plainly that it was easier to begin a war than to end one, and that the power and resources of the tribes together was no match for the Americans. He said that an Indian league would be but a weak cord to unite their interest and that it was a frenzied undertaking without a solid foundation and must fall inevitably with its own weakness.[73]

In order to establish his peaceable disposition with Colonel Hawkins and to make an atonement for his past folly, the Big Warrior advised the killing of Tecumseh, as a propagator of mischief among them. He thought a public execution of Tecumseh, with a full explanation of the reason for the execution, would stop the mad proceedings.

But when he expressed his opinion in the Creek council house, it was shocking to many of the chiefs. They said the perpetration of such a deed seemed wrong and unprecedented to them. By such a deed they would lose the faith of all nations, as Tecumseh had come to them as a friendly man to a friendly nation and had done nothing to them worthy of death. Their advice was that he and his talks might go away in peace, which would keep them clear of his blood. Tecumseh took his leave of them to see if he could infuse mischief in other tribes.

As Tecumseh's calm and determined manner and independence was the admiration of the Ispocoga tribe, they could not but venerate his prophetic way of delivering his speeches, which he did without any doubt of their accomplishment. What he said, he implied, was dictated to him by the Great Spirit, of whose will he acted as the mere organ. In this way he proselyted many who thought his singular manner of relating omens and predictions worthy of imitation.

Captain Isaacs

So the age of prophecy in the Creek nation displaced the light of reason and knowledge for a time. Many turned prophets, which was a prelude to mad and diabolical actions, all attributed to inspiration. The prophets went so far as to pretend to have frequent and long conversations with the great Master of Breath upon topics related to the future. These pretended dialogues soon became a matter of destruction to many well-meaning and peaceful people. For a man to express the least doubt of a prophet's being inspired was to insure he would become a victim of prophetic wrath. The prophets made the community at large subservient to the prophetic mandates, whether the people believed in them or not.

In their prophetic incantations they could know who were witches and who dealt with evil-disposed spirits. The people generally would believe such, as they are superstitious. A man would be announced to be acquainted with the diabolical art for such actions as flying about the country to poison people who were inimical to him, blowing a contagious air into a house in passing by it at night, blowing into the nostrils and lungs of a person he did not like when asleep, causing instant death. Witches were said to be seen at twilight only, flying about to do mischief. Whenever such a person was found, he was seized by a mob and tied to a tree with ropes; light wood was piled around him and set on fire. He was burned to death with as little compunction or remorse as in the Roman Inquisition. Many people who were enlightened and disposed to peace and order were brought to this fiery ordeal. All this was done so that the fanatics and evil-disposed might reign undisturbed. No council that did not suit the disposition of the times was tolerated before the public.

In these wild happenings Captain Isaacs played a conspicuous part.[74] He began as a conjurer, representing his skill and knowledge in the art of enchantment as unequalled. If he was so minded, he would petrify anyone who opposed or thwarted him. He continually related the wonderful things he could do and the miraculous things

The Shawnee prophet, Tenskwetawa, pictured here with his sacred string of beads and fire stick, was Tecumseh's brother. A group of Coosawda Creeks came under the Prophet's power when they visited in the Ohio Valley, before Tecumseh came south in 1811 trying to persuade the southern tribes to help drive white settlers off Indian land.

Reprinted from ROYAL B. HASSRICK, THE GEORGE CATLIN BOOK OF AMERICAN INDIANS, *p. 41.* PROMONTORY PRESS, NEW YORK, 1981.

he had done. He told of having dived down to the bottom of the river and lying there and traveling about for many days and nights receiving instruction and information from an enormous and friendly serpent that dwelt there and was acquainted with future events and all other things necessary for a man to know in this life.

By such tales Captain Isaacs's art was dreaded, and by the foolish herd his person held in superstitious veneration. He and all the other divine pretenders were induced to do their wonder workings by Tecumseh's influence. The Indians were certain that the shaking of the earth, which happened near the time of Tecumseh's speech, was done by Tecumseh. Their conviction left no room to doubt anything he had said of the successful irruption of the Indians against the white people. They thought it madness not to wage a war to expel the white people from their lands and rightful country, an action willed by the great Master of Breath.

When the prophets began their fanatical preparations for a general war, the Big Warrior was apprehensive. Seeing events going from bad to worse, he thought it advisable to fortify himself and his followers in Tuckabatchee, to be ready for any hostile movement that might be made against him.[75] He expected that the prophets would attempt to do something against him, as he dissented from their plans of war. About the time that he commenced fortifying, the adjacent townspeople had assembled at Othlewallee, or Cluwallee, above the mouth of Line Creek and began an entrenched camp. The whole nation was in commotion and excited, and not one of them could tell why. All the information they could collect or hear by assembling or inquiring of each other was that the ferment and agitation was a general thing, progressing from bad to worse, by and through the prophetic men. As the number of prophets increased, they vied with each other in excelling in wild predictions and adducing the most romantic circumstances of a frivolous nature to confirm it as a divine call.

The prophets circulated reports of their frequent interviews with the great Giver, or Taker, of Breath. By such reports [they hoped to] raise their fame so as to gain the ascendancy over the multitude and awe them into submission to their will.

As an instance of this and to awe the people, Josiah Francis,[76] a half-blooded Frenchman, who was of the prophets, claimed to have received an order from the Master of Breath to meet him every day at a certain place, as he intended to teach him the different languages that he would want to use, and writing, so that he could transmit his own and the national affairs without applying for such assistance to another person. According to the divine injunction, Francis absented himself every day as if for his instruction, which many believed to be the case. In a short time he informed his adherents that he was learned in writing and languages, perfect enough to converse, write, and do his own business.

The next thing was to convince them of such a miracle by showing them of it, so that his divine favor might never be doubted. He wrote a lengthy letter in Spanish (a language of which he knew not a word) to the government at Pensacola, requesting them to send arms, of which he stood in great need to carry on hostilities

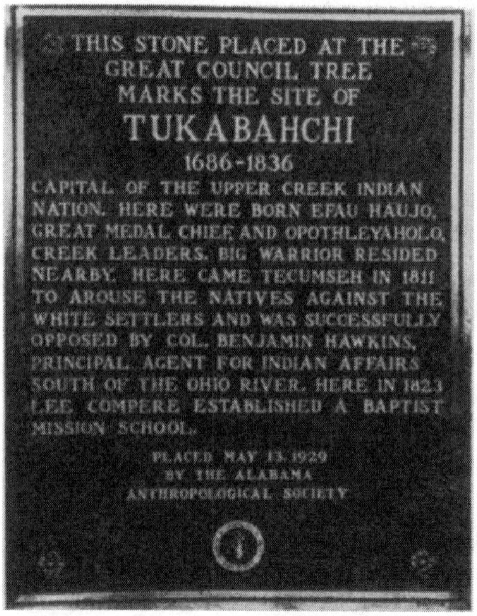

A marker on a boulder in a Tallassee, Alabama, city park, commemorates Tuckabatchee, the Upper Creek capital on the Tallapoosa River. (Photograph courtesy of ALABAMA DEPARTMENT OF ARCHIVES AND HISTORY*)*

against the Americans. He gave his envoys a full, detailed account of the contents of the letter, by reading and interpreting it to them in a precise manner. (In their way of ridiculing his presumption they have since said that his letter looked more like a paper full of crooked marks than writing.) They carried it, nevertheless, to the governor, as they had to do for fear of their lives. When the governor opened the letter and asked them the reason why such a paper of marks was sent to him, their opinion of the legible writing was verified. The governor declared that it contained not a letter of writing. They saw that he was angry about it and wished to exculpate themselves of passing a slur on him by giving him such a paper. They satisfied him by detailing to him all that Francis had said was contained in the letter. Seeing their simplicity, the governor had no doubt of their innocence.

When they finished relating to him all of Francis's mad deeds and sayings, he laughed heartily and ridiculed Francis for pretending to write. He said he had a notion to return him a letter in answer of the same unintelligible writing informing him that he had no arms or munitions of war for him. So the envoys returned home without arms or munitions.

Josiah Francis and Paddy Walsh, seeing themselves put in the background by the rising fame of Captain Isaacs, wanted to emulate him and cast him down from the pinnacle of his fame so that after his fall they might retain between them an ascendancy over the multitude, whom they intended to domineer by prophet craft. As a beginning to his downfall they pretended to have divine information that Isaacs in his conjurations and ominous revelations got his information from a familiar diabolical spirit who had taught him a singular way of diving into the water and flying through the air for mischievous purposes. [They also charged] that he had power to injure or destroy anyone that he pleased, provided they did not use salt victuals; that some witches were disposed to good toward man, and some bad, and that Isaac's friend was of the latter class. So he was pronounced a diabolical witch. The community proscribed him, and his portion was to be death by fire, to cleanse his body of the pollution that was attached to him because of his wicked practices.

Some of Isaacs's adherents were so truly and reverently attached to him that they resolved to share his precarious fortunes with him. They let him know of his impending fate and of the great defection of his party. They held a consultation of what to do to insure his and their safety, and they decided to put themselves at the mercy of the Tuckabatchees, who, they expected, were more consistent than those they were about to leave. Accordingly, they joined their interests with the Big Warrior in his fort with a full resolve to share both good and bad fortune with the Tuckabatchees.

It was an unfortunate circumstance for the hostile camps that when Isaacs fled he did not forget the powder and lead he had on hand, but was mindful to carry it with him thinking that it would make him welcome with his new party [Tuckabatchees] that heretofore had no friendship with him. In his calculation he was not mistaken, as the Tuckabatchees were very much in want of powder and lead. Therefore, his arrival with ammunition and a reinforcement of Tuskegee and Coosawda fugitives was hailed with a hearty welcome. Both his return to reason and his defection from his late friends were highly extolled.

The scare that Captain Isaacs got in the camp of his late party which caused his flight to the Big Warrior was what saved the Tuckabatchees: First, there was the acquisition of his powder and lead, their supplies of which were too scant for a battle or a siege. Second, the reinforcement brought by Captain Isaacs gave the fort more strength by augmenting their force to six hundred effective men for war. It was never acertained what the force of the hostile camp was, as there never was a time when all were in camp at once, but the hostile band numbered 4,800.[77] These were dreadful odds when two forces in mortal enmity were within eight miles of each other.

The flight that Captain Isaacs made to save his life caused a great uproar in the hostile camp; there was irritation that a witch known to be of the worst kind should escape their just vengeance. They collected their whole force and made an immediate attack on the Tuckabatchee fort, but they were repulsed with considerable loss. They made an attack every day for some days. With daily loss of men, and without making an impression on the fort, they then laid siege to it, thinking to starve it to surrender. The hostiles were determined to take the fortress so that they might have the fugitive witch once more in their power, to torture him to death with fire and splinters of light wood and recover much needed power.

Big Warrior

It was soon known over the whole nation that the hostile attacks on the Big Warrior fort had turned to a siege. When the Cowetas of Chattahoochee found out the situation of the Tuckabatchees, they sent a large force to their relief under the control of Joseph Marshall, who went into the fort through the river line of the hostile camps.[78] The second day after the entry of the reinforcement, the hostile band decided to make another, final effort on the fort, to crush the opposing party at a blow. Early in the day they made an assault up to the very pickets, where they were received in so deadly a manner that many of them, to escape being killed, lay down as though they were dead. Braver ones lay down and rolled over to the pickets and tried to cut their opponents down. But after an assault supported for some time by mortal hatred, they retreated, not as men beaten off, but as men daring the besieged to follow them.

The Tuckabatchees must have felt themselves roughly handled, for the Big Warrior and Marshall the next day started for the state of Georgia. Women and children, mixed with armed men, marched out of the fort in a line for the river and crossed it. The men in the rear, stripped to their naked bodies and painted red, black, or white, were ready and willing to fight for their wives and children. Their determined manner must have dampened the ardor of the hostiles, for they never molested them or pursued them on the road. So they had no interruption in their escape to Georgia.

In the assault on the fort, Marshall lost one of his eyes by a bullet wound on his eyeball.

I never could find anyone who conjectured regarding the number killed and lost of the two parties. But I would suppose the losses of the hostile party were considerable; the Big Warrior could not have made such an easy escape had the hostiles not been considerably crippled, and they would have made one more attempt to capture Captain Isaacs.

So ended the siege that caused the Big Warrior to abandon the nation to the hostile band, a siege instigated by the fanatical, self-made prophet and upheld by the deluded multitude. This was the commencement of that civil and general war which was prosecuted in a ruthless manner for no cause, until the Creek or Ispocoga tribe was devastated.

It may be observed from the aforesaid period that the result of all their undertakings was that misfortune had selected them for her darling, had nurtured them in scenes of misguided afflictions, and had destined them to seal their fate (however disapproved by them in the wild forests of the West) after being the thoroughfare of every series of practical villainy that was ever heard of or thought of before or to be hereafter.

THE CREEK WAR

When the Big Warrior was rescued by Marshall and the Cowetas, and when he quit and gave up the nation to the hostile party and took shelter in the state of Georgia, it was plain that the die was cast. Nothing would turn up but a civil and general war to terminate their differences and establish their different views. As yet, some only contemplated the destruction of the Big Warrior, Captain Isaacs and their party, while others were for pillage and war on all that opposed their way, white men or Indians. The latter opinion preponderated, and the entrenchment of the hostile camp was enlarged and extended so as to embrace two parts of the Othlewallee, both sides of the Tallapoosa River near the mouth of Line Creek.[79]

While the hostiles stayed in camp they felt free and lived plentifully on beef. As the stock holders were mostly gone, they wantonly killed all the cattle in the nation and negligently wasted the meat that would have supported them many months with economy and a little care. By their extravagance they soon came to near starvation.

While their camps were in a state of plenty, it was the continual resort of the hostile band, for all others were interdicted by a say of the prophets. The prophets pretended that a man of a contrary opinion could not impose himself on them; they said they could tell, as quickly as they touched any part of him, who was opposed to their measures, or who ate salt victuals. On shaking hands with any man of this description, the prophet instantly began trembling; the defilement subsided by a gradual jerking of all his muscles. . . . During the agitation he did not appear to labor under any effort to [achieve this jerking], but he certainly did it with a strain on his nerves and by habitual practice.[80]

Burnt Corn Battle

. . . As Captain Isaacs had saved himself from the hostiles' vengeance, taking his powder and lead, leaving them destitute of the essential article, it was necessary to have some, and that was to be procured only from their Spanish friends in Pensacola. It was the only place they dared to approach to get any. A body of 280 men started for Pensacola, headed by their most prophetic man, High-headed Jim, or Cusseta Tustenuggee.[81]

On July 7, 1813, on their way down to Pensacola, at Burnt Corn Springs, the hostile Creeks charged the house of James Cornels. Cornels was not at home, and they took Mrs. Cornels and a man called Marler and carried them on to Pensacola with them. They sold them there as prisoners of war to citizens of the place, who gave the Indians a small price to get them out of their possession.

When the Creeks attacked Cornels's house, their inroad was so unexpected that they had it completely in their power to make a general sweep of the country down to the present town of Stockton. Fortunately for the country it was saved because the Indians miscalculated what happened. At the taking of Mrs. Cornels, the Indians were so intent in plundering the house that they never noticed a couple of Negroes about the place who ran off toward the river settlement about fifteen miles away. When they realized that an hour later, they sent in pursuit of the Negroes to the next house, but they were gone. They were sure that the man who lived there would speed to the river and give an alarm before they could reach there in pursuit with a force sufficient to do anything. It proved otherwise than was calculated. The running Negroes told the white man of the Indian descent on the country, thinking he would inform the river settlement of the danger. But he cared only for his safety and mounted his small family on horseback and made into the woods for security. Had the Indians continued their pursuit of the Negroes they would have overtaken them before they reached the next house. But the Indians did not, because of their prophet's advice. So the Negroes gave the alarm when they got to the next man's house. This man was not so selfish or careful of his horses as the first man. All his thoughts were to warn his friends of their danger so that they might extricate themselves by a timely flight, which they did.

Immediately after Mrs. Cornels's capture, all those inhabiting the lower part of the state on the eastern bank [of the Alabama River], both Indians and white people, repaired with all their movables to a place known as the Cut Off,[82] bordering and in the white settlement. There, after consultation, the Indian refugees and inhabitants of the place decided on the propriety of fortifying against a future irruption of the hostile Indians and erected the ever memorable Fort Mims.

About the time Fort Mims was completed, James Caller, the colonel of the country, mustered all the men he could, numbering about 180, part Indians and part white men. The purpose of the expedition was to meet the Indians who went to Pensacola and on their return to give them battle and take powder and lead if they should have any.

The colonel and his guides made a circuitous route without seeing any Indians and were nearly out of expectation of meeting any, until they arrived at a branch of Burnt Corn Creek in Conecuh County. There they saw about a half dozen Indians in the swamp. As quick as they could they charged and ran them back to the swamp. There were already about sixty men in the swamp. When they had painted themselves for battle, they came out of the swamp and made a hideous and yelling attack on the colonel's assailing corps. Although there were sixty Indians, they had but thirteen guns among them. The unarmed ones assisted during the action by whooping and encouraging the armed men, which was all they could do in their circumstances. What few guns they had was enough to gain a decisive and almost bloodless victory.

When the Indians came out of the swamp with the charge and war whoop, the colonel's men were panic-stricken and made a quick retreat, which soon became a flight so intense that many never fired a gun, though the colonel sent some of his officers on fleet horses to gain their front and remonstrate with them on their unmanly conduct and to return and fight. In spite of all arguments to the contrary they kept on in the same speed; their panic was greater than the honor of their country.

The white people lost five men killed and as many wounded. Among the latter was Colonel Sam Dale, who got shot in one shoulder. The Indians lost two and a Negro killed and five wounded. The Negro killed was making his escape from the Indians to the white people for their protection.[83]

The victory gained by the hostile party, almost without having to fight, proved their own overthrow. It gave them an exalted opinion of their own valor and prowess and a most contemptible opinion of the Americans who, they were confident, were touched by a cowardly spirit by the will of the Master of Breath, so that they would have less trouble in destroying them.

After their attack on the Cornels house, the hostiles had decided not to stay and fight the whites on the river settlement, but since their object was a supply of ammunition, to proceed on to Pensacola. When the hostiles got there they demanded an interview with the governor and intendant. The governor thought that the town was in a critical situation, having few soldiers to guard it when there were nearly three hundred Indians in it so intent on war that they begged or demanded ammunition, throwing out oblique hints of what they might do in case they were compelled to act. At length the governor gave them a private audience, but it was never known if they agreed on any plan, as the interpreter would never tell of such a thing. By some unknown means the Creeks got several horseloads of powder and lead, which they carried off. After this they always got their supplies of ammunition at Pensacola, whether from the government authorities or citizens it is unknown. But I never doubted there was a general concern on the part of authorities and citizens to sell or give the Indians as much ammunition as they wanted whenever they called for it.

Before the Indians left Pensacola to go home, Colonel Caller had called for volunteers in order to give them battle, expressly to get their powder. At that time, several men who were acquainted with many of the Indians went down to Pensacola under a pretext of seeing what they were about and what their intentions were. It was suspected by many that these men had made some agreement with the Indians to spare them and their property in future inroads into their country. In return they would give the hostiles news of anything agitated against them by the white people. They were suspected of giving a full detail of what Colonel Caller aimed. The Indians say they were informed of the movements made by the Americans to intercept their ammunition, but they would not say who their informant was. As they received full light on the American movement and intentions, they thought it best to divide their squadron into many gangs, by which measure their ammunition would have more chances to reach home. It was one of these parties that defeated Colonel Caller's corps of volunteers.

At their arrival back at the hostile camps, the Indians told in a vaunting manner of defeating an immense army of Americans and running them from the field of battle; as proof they displayed scalps in a victory dance. Then and there it was announced that they would take revenge on that part of the state for the unprovoked attack on them. They had a long-standing desire to try their strength with that part of the present state for imposing on them for many years. They had been obliged to land every time they passed by Fort Stoddart on the Tombigbee River. They looked on this as a grievance, and felt spite to that part of the state. . . .

William Weatherford

In some of the following occurrences William Weatherford will appear on the stage of action, a man who has been celebrated as a leader of the hostile band. But to this period he had been shy of them and had no concern in their cabals, either directly or indirectly. But fate so ordered his fortune that he was drawn into the war measures of the hostile party in an unpremeditated way, and contrary to his opinion of such foolish undertakings. He abhorred their wicked proceedings, though he afterwards participated in a conspicuous manner in their war measures. As long as he could get followers, nothing could have been farther in his opinion than that he would ever join in their hostile measures. When the hostiles began their fanatical riots of shaving their heads and painting them red for distinction, making encampments and destroying the inoffensive, peaceable, and well inclined, he could not but feel thoughtful and doubt his personal safety should they continue their riotous ways. But he concluded from their action in general that the storm of their frenzied delusion was in full blast and would blow off like a tornado in a short time. They would retract their self-deluded errors and become more calm, sociable, and less devilish toward each other.

In order to keep clear of being implicated in his words or actions, Weatherford made it his business to make a trip to Pensacola to get some necessaries for his family consumption. While he was absent down to Pensacola, his wife's kinsmen removed his wife and all his movable property to the hostile camps at Othlewallee (which was considered as hostile headquarters), above the mouth of Line Creek. On returning home from Pensacola he was surprised and perplexed to find his family and property forced into the camps of the ferocious hostile band. He knew not what to do. To leave his family and property in the hostiles' mercy and go down the river to his relatives seemed like parting soul and body. At length he concluded on a plan to fool them. To effect his purpose, he thought it advisable to hide his disapproval of what they had done, and patiently await a fit opportunity to run off with his family and property from under the eyes of the hostile bands. He repaired to the hostile camp expecting to effect his plan of reprisal, but he had no chance to escape with his family before the Burnt Corn battle. After that it proved too late for him to withdraw with safety on either side.[84]

Before the Burnt Corn battle it was known to many of his friends and acquaintances that Weatherford had entered the hostile camps, and his reason for doing this was likewise known to them. . . . Yet for all that, when the hostiles were vanquished in battle at Burnt Corn, in the heat of their rage the vanquished party swore his death on sight, for no other reason than they knew he was at that time in hostile camps. They knew he had taken no part in the hostiles' activities or debates for the extension of their raids on the frontier settlers. Weatherford knew of the threats put out against him, and who made them, and that the threats seemed to be made by determined men with determined intent. This he got from runaway Negroes who joined the hostile Indians to assist in exterminating the white people and be free.

As the hostile band was ready to commence active operations and depradations on their foe, it was necessary for Weatherford to be decisive about his critical and dangerous situation. He could see no other way to extricate himself with any safety of person and property. To leave his wife and children and effects in the hands of the vigilant hostile band, to make his escape, and to fly to those who were his sworn and deathly enemies seemed but folly and madness. He could devise no way to explain the reason for his conduct to his former friends and to elude the vigilance of the hostile party so as not to be found out by them. If detected in an attempt to leave, he knew death was his portion, and probably of his whole family.

The hostiles noticed some appearance of uneasiness and a coldness in him toward their measures, and they appeared to keep an unusually strict eye on him and his conduct. They had gone so far in their distrust as to accuse him of dissimulation and disaffection to the common cause. It was hard to clear himself of the circulating report of his joining the hostile party, as he had stayed in the hostile camps so long, which he did awaiting an efficient chance to escape with what he had. At length he ascertained positively that his conduct was implicated irretrievably with his former friends and acquaintances and he himself proscribed by those he once considered as unalterable friends. Convinced that such was his present standing, he had no choice left but to stay with his family and make the best of a bad recourse by taking his fate in the hostile ranks.

Before he gave up the idea of an elopement with his family, the hostile party held a general council to know what was best to be done, as they were then ready to commence their extermination of the white people. It was concluded to go down the river and make an attack on Fort Mims and Fort Pierce;[85] they were about two miles apart. Their whole aim was to humble and destroy Fort Mims; they knew there were a great many men in there who had fought at Burnt Corn. As they wanted all the advice they could obtain on the propriety of such a descent on that place, Weatherford's opinion was asked for the first time by both the leaders of bands and by the prophets (who descended to ask advice of mortal man). They wished to pay deference to his views on the practicability of making an impression on their hated Fort Mims. Because Weatherford knew their determination and that they could not be biased by him to stop and to divert their views to some other place as an object worthy of their attention, he gave them his opinion without reserve: he thought an attack might be made with success. They thought he delivered his sentiments without reserve. As a result, there was a sudden transition in their minds from threats and distrust of his integrity in their cause to an unbounded confidence and reliance in him. . . .

Their future operations were left entirely to Weatherford's guidance and control. The prophets accordingly submitted themselves to his opinion and directed others to do likewise. Paddy Walsh, one of their prophets, was nominated to the office of head leader.[86] Though he acted as head, he acted under the influence of Weatherford's opinion.

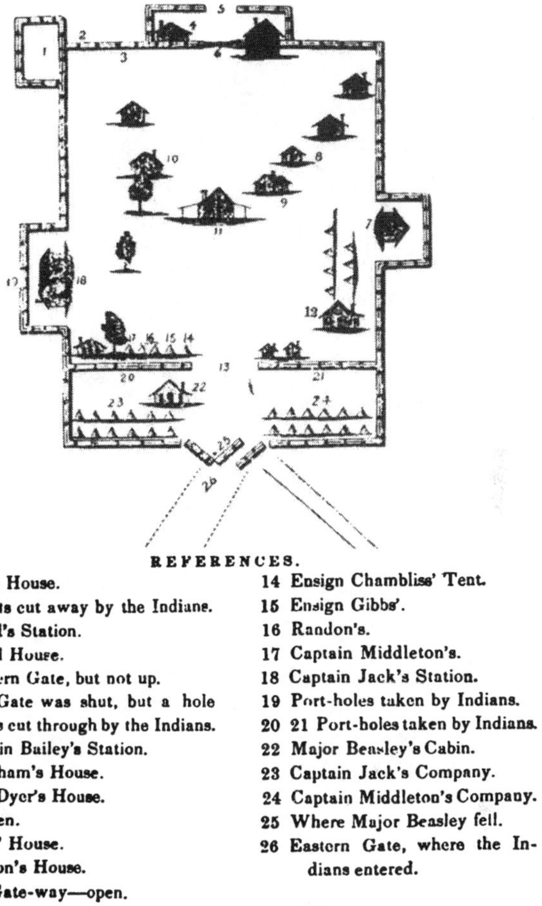

A drawing of Fort Mims found among General Claiborne's papers.
(Photograph courtesy of ALABAMA DEPARTMENT OF ARCHIVES AND HISTORY*)*

Fort Mims

The day was set for all the forces to concentrate at the mouth of Flat Creek, and they sent the broken days to all the towns. The "broken days" is a bundle of broken parts of twigs about four inches long, every piece for one day, tied carefully in a bundle; one stick is thrown away at sunrise every day until the last, which is the day appointed. On the appointed day the leaders of different towns collected the warriors of every town separately and held a war dance. After it was over they started on different routes for the mouth of Flat Creek in Monroe County, where they were to concentrate their whole force, numbering 726 effective warriors. Before they moved from there they held their great war dance.

In making their descent on the fort, they did not move with the dispatch which is generally supposed. They were four days going about fifty miles. In this time they were seen frequently by different persons out to see their plantations, some as far as twenty-five miles from the fort. [The whites] returned in haste and told where they had seen a great many Indians mounted and on foot, that they were on the road that led directly to the fort, and that their number appeared immense because they could only see one end of them in single file. The informers were generally men of Fort Pierce, so their report was disbelieved, expecting it was told to give them unnecessary alarm for the defense of their own fort. Also, it could not be supposed by those acquainted with the Indian mode of warfare that they would presume to attack a regular fortification knowing it was defended by 139 men, the force at Fort Mims. A few Indians and several Indian Negroes who had run away from Fort Pierce to the nation informed both Indians and Weatherford of the force of each fort and who particularly resided in each fort. Weatherford was likewise informed of the continued hard threats put out against him and by whom they were made.

The day before the Fort Mims assault, the whole band of Indians stopped about six miles from the fort, in the after part of the day to cool and refresh themselves. At that time they saw two mounted men or scouts in another road about three hundred yards distance; they were seemingly careless and in deep conversation. . . . From their manner of riding they appeared to be under no perceptible alarm, so the Indians were confident that the men had not seen their trail. Many of the Indians, however, urged a pursuit of the men to cut them off; but they were not allowed to do it, on the inference that the men had not seen their trail. If they cut them off from the fort and in the pursuit killed them, their not returning to the fort would cause an alarm and search, which would cause the Indians to be seen. And if they escaped from their pursuit it would be the same. If they were allowed to go on, on their safe return to the fort they would undoubtedly report there was no enemy to be seen. The report of the scouts would ensure security and carelessness at the fort. When they were assaulted they would be unaware of it and in an unprepared state. This proved to be a fact.

The Indian band, not expecting any more scouts on that road, went on deliberately after the men, to about three-quarters of a mile of the fort, where they halted for the night, to refresh themselves for tomorrow's work. After dark and all things were still, Weatherford selected two men that he could confide in and depend on in case of danger. With them he went to view the plan and reconnoiter the fort and its exact situation. He pushed his examination of the fort so far that he and one of his men got to the pickets and looked through the portholes, which was easily done for they were four feet high and about four feet apart all around, without ditch or bank. They gained very little insight by their looking through the portholes, as there but a few glimmering lights scattered about. All looked so obscure and gloomy that Weatherfod saw little of the interior situation of the fort. But in getting to the fort unperceived he judged that they were careless and negligent in guarding the fort; and as they were moving about in a careless manner and conversing on common topics of life he was sure that the scouts had not seen the Indians or given any alarm. After trying to see what he could in the fort, he and his men returned to the army, who by day were informed of his operations at the fort.

The leaders of bands assisted Weatherford in digesting the plan of attack. Every man, painted red or black and stripped to the buff, knew the part and place he was to act in. As a necessary measure for their successful assault, Paddy Walsh urged, because the field surrounding the fort was large, that they run up to the wall without firing a gun and take possession of the portholes. As that was being done, four men that he would select and make invulnerable against white men's bullets were to enter the fort and fight inside as long as they thought fit. Their safe retreat out of the fort was to be an omen to the Indians that they were to take the place. Accordingly, when the others ran up to the walls, the four selected men ran in at the gate, raised the war scream, and penetrated to the very center. All got killed but one, and he quickly retreated without a hurt. He was of Jim Boy's town; for his prowess in performing that action, on his arrival at home at the war dance he got the war name of Na-ho-mah-tee O-thle-ho-bo-yer,[87] which is "the foremost man in danger, in the time of battle."

All their prognostics being arranged and made known and all the men in readiness, the army divided in three divisions. They silently moved on to the attack of the fort on August 30, 1813. While they were trying to take a view of the fort and anxiously waiting, the fort drum beat for twelve o'clock. The Indians were sure they had been seen, and that it was an alarm drum. The word was given to charge. The whole body started in full speed for the fort. Though they were a large body, they were less than a hundred yards from the fort gate before they were seen by anyone. The gate sentry was engaged in looking over the shoulders of a couple playing cards. The Indians ran up and raised the war whoop and took possession of three squares of the fort and of the ill-constructed portholes, which were just high enough for their use.

There was a cry in the fort, "The Indians, the Indians." All seemed in confusion. No one was ready. As they got ready and came out of their houses, they were mostly killed by the Indians from the portholes. The year troops with Major Beasley, who commanded all, were killed in a few minutes. There was a dividing wall in the fort, and the year troops had one division of it. What remained of the year troops ran into the other part that was occupied by the militia and families. Though the Indians made their assault with steadiness and seeming desperation, they were twice repelled by the brave white men and Indians within. The Indians set on fire all the houses near the east wall; the fire soon progressed to the dwellings that stood in the center, and so on. So those within were compelled to fight in desperation when they found themselves surrounded by smoke and dire, death-dealing bullets, and the unceasing echo of the war whoop. The Indians found themselves so roughly handled that they drew off for nearly an hour; they would not have commenced their attack anew, but the Negroes they had would not cease, urging them on by reciting that they thought it interested them to have the fort destroyed. The Indians were urged on to the charge and renewed the attack.

The people within sustained their fort against the assailants until about an hour of sun setting, when the heat of the houses on fire became so intense in the narrow space, and the want of water so great, that their position was unsupportable. At that time their men were greatly thinned. Besides, there were but two houses and a tent for shelter from the enemy, as all the rest were on fire or burned down. No attempt could be made to get water from the well without being killed, as the Indians had possession of the portholes. As their situation allowed them no chance, and it was their wish to sell their lives at as dear a rate as possible, it was concluded to cut the pickets down at the bent and go out of the fort and die fighting in the field, where the women and children might have a chance to escape. The pickets were cut down accordingly and they all went out simultaneously. When out, no one stayed to fight, but every man tried to make his escape to the thicket and swamps.

On the day before the fort was attacked, there was a general muster of the men in the fort, when there appeared to be 76 year troops and 52 effective militia and 11 unfit for duty, making 139 men in all. Of the aforesaid men 17 made their escape. One hundred and twenty-two were killed; besides them 201 women and children were killed. The whole posse of the fort—men, women, and children—at the time of the assault numbered 340. Of that number 11 were taken out alive as prisoners of war. This leaves the number massacred 303. A total of 28 escaped or were taken prisoners.

The hostile Indians' loss at the fort, by computations made by heads of towns, was thus: such as died of their wounds, 202; many that got wounded survived. It was reported that the great reduction in their ranks by death, wounds, and other disabilities that they got in taking Fort Mims was what caused them not to attempt anything at that time against Fort Pierce. But many of the Indians, as well as white people, supposed it was by some prior understanding made with some people in Fort Pierce.

When the people in Fort Mims began to cut down the pickets to make their escape out, Weatherford was near with several others who understood their language. From what he heard the whites say, he judged that his mortal enemies were sufficiently humbled. He undoubtedly knew the horrible doom that awaited the white people when once they were out of the fort and in the Indians' power. He further knew the Indian mode of war when they overpowered their enemy in battle. He would willingly have saved from death by intercession such of them as he was desirous of saving. When he thought of their sorrowing and jeopardized situation, he did not stay to witness the catastrophe awaiting them. His manly breast that he had unshrinkingly exposed to their death-dealing rifle balls during the eventful day was all at once filled with sorrowing reflections, for some he knew to be there were his dearest friends. His eyes refused to see their mangled end. He turned for his horse, mounted him abruptly, and rode off for his brother David Tate's plantation without deigning to look back.

The night after the conflagration of the fort and the massacre of the people, and after the hostiles had gathered all the horses and other property they could find, they then had time to reflect on their dear-bought achievement in taking the fort. Behold, when they stated their position, they found that of their men that went into action fully half were killed or disabled or wounded. They could no longer stand the deception of their prophet and commanding leader. Paddy Walsh had assured them that when they commenced the assault he would run around the fort three times. After he had done that, the force of the bullets shot from the fort would be dead or fly upwards, none of the Indians would be killed, and they would have nothing to do but draw their knives and war clubs, enter the fort, and slay all in it without fear or danger, as all the men would be in a state of torpitude and paralyzed. Paddy Walsh did as he said he would. He ran around the fort three times, but he was shot down. However, he kept encouraging his men to throw down their firearms and enter the fort with war clubs and scalping knives in hand. Those that were inside the fort defied the hostiles to do it, saying it was what they wished them to try as they were prepared for such a measure. No doubt that kept them from trying that event.

Fort Sinquefield

When the hostiles had all got together again, they saw the consequences of the dear-bought conquest. They rose in fury against the prophet and leading man, Paddy Walsh, for their losing so many men by death and wounds. Though he had himself been shot through the body in three places, it did not excuse him. The Alabamas, to get him out of the hands of the infuriated populace, took canoes and transported him and themselves up the river to Towassee town, as he was of that clan. The town stood in the bend of the river below the city of Montgomery in Montgomery County. They traveled so slowly home by water that all the wounded were cured.

As they traveled they continually reconnoitered the country. On the west side of the Alabama River they found a fort and decided to take and sack it. The duty of leading the enterprise fell on the Dog Warrior, called by the Alabamas Coole-jer, which in English is "light maker."[88] He took a detachment of between ninety and one hundred men and moved directly to Fort Sinquefield and made an assault on it. From the reports of his reconnoitering parties, he had no doubt of taking it easily. But to his surprise and mortification the fort had got a reinforcement, gave him a warm reception, and repulsed him with a loss of nine of his men. Five were killed in the attack and four died of their wounds afterwards.[89] This attempt on Fort Sinquefield closed the scenes of their first uprising on the Tensaw settlement.

The hostile party got a vast number of horses and a great deal of other effects in their pillage of Fort Mims and the surrounding country. They thereby concluded that the time had arrived, spoken of by Tecumseh and repeatedly confirmed after that by their own prophets, that there was to come a time when the Indians would have sole possession and undisturbed range of all their lands and country. No white man would dare put his foot thereon without their permission. Such was decreed by the Great Spirit, and it must come to pass and so remain.

Holy Ground

Not being a warrior, Josiah Francis had not joined Weatherford and Paddy Walsh in the Fort Mims attack. He pretended to be very busy erecting a town on a parcel of ground that he said was pointed out to him, a spot made sacred by the Great Spirit and consecrated solely for the Indians. It was never to be sullied by the footsteps of the white man. A destructive barrier circled all around it, which a white man could not pass over alive. Francis hoped to populate the town with permanent settlers such as had quit the camps at Othlewallee, which was almost turned into a Babel because of a confusion of languages during the hostiles' stay together. Francis announced that his place had been named Ekon-achaka, which in English is "sacred or beloved ground."[90] . . .

After their victorious expedition and return home, the hostile Indians vaunted mightily of their deed and made a great display of their plundered wealth to those that had stayed home in ease and idleness. These were mostly Francis's adherents; they could not but see their own poverty and the sudden wealth of the opposite party. On reflection they began to say that they would have such affluence had they not followed the idle advice of Francis to stay at home and build the sacred town. They rightly blamed his stay and wanting to build on nothing but a pretext to hide his fear and cowardice. So he was becoming contemptible among his adherents as well as to the other party. He knew from the recent massacre at Fort Mims that there were no enemy left to annoy him. Francis understood from Negro prisoners that there were many horses in the Tensaw River fields that could be got by going far. He told his men that by his foreknowledge he could tell them that if they would follow him they would get nearly as much booty and property as the other party. Accordingly there followed him to the gleaning upwards of 108 war men, who gathered all the horses that were overlooked and left by the other party and burned all the dwelling houses, sawmills, etc. They dug up and destroyed an immense quantity of household furniture, being shown by the Negro prisoners where such had been buried by their former owners on their going to the unfortunate fortress.

Francis carried out his expedition, never encountering an enemy, and returned covered with laurels of glory. By making the expedition he gained ascendancy over the community of his original townsmen and got them into his holy town. Many who lived in the vicinity were persuaded to go into the town because they heard that the white people were on the alert, raising troops on the Tombigbee side from the west, an armament the hostiles knew must be for the purpose of chastising them for their horrid deeds and depradations. As their town was next to the white settlement, it received runaway Negroes who confirmed the story of the American armament. But they carelessly carried on their town buildings without seeming to mind such reports. Near Christmas they were informed by one of their swift lookout men that he had seen near the town of Claiborne a large army of white men moving up the river on the big road. This report was confirmed by the runners every day for four days. On the fourth day they were attacked by General Claiborne.[91] They returned the general's salute for one round and began to give way and cross the river with their prophet at their head to seek safety on the other side. They saw that the white people had crossed Francis's enchanted death-dealing barrier around their town. His adherents were shaken in their hitherto firm reliance on their prophet's foresight. They fled after him from the place where they had awaited the attack of the enemy, in the woods bordering the Holy Ground town. Seeing their white pursuers pass the enchanted line without dropping dead, they perceived that their purifications and incantations of the night before were not strong enough to save them and the Holy Ground from destruction. The prophet led the way and showed them how to escape danger by flight and by swimming. They did not fight for his holy-made ground and dwelling.

Though the prophet and his party who lived on the Holy Ground left the field of battle and made their escape, the fighting contention did not cease with their running off with the loss of a few warriors. For William Weatherford kept it up a while longer.

Weatherford happened there by chance in this way. He and McPherson, a Scotch and Indian half-breed, heard from a runner a few days before the attack that he had seen an army of white men, both on horses and on foot, coming up the road. Weatherford, McPherson, and their friends, who lived on the big road, concluded it was not safe to stay there. They would go to the Big Swamp creek and to the Holy Ground town. There they would be off the big road and be in more force in the town when invaded, as they were sure that an attack was intended by the white army.

As they purposed to reinforce Francis and his followers by moving to his town, Weatherford went with three others and took a closer view of the approaching army, about two miles from the town. He knew that the Indians were in no way able to withstand such a force and equipment. He returned and made preparations to repel them, if possible, with a force of about two hundred men. When the war men of the town heard of their approach and went in array to meet them, Weatherford, McPherson, and their neighbors (about thirty men) joined with them. They and the runaway Negroes were all determined; they meant to give the foe as good a fight as possible.

After the defection and total desertion of Francis and his followers, it was the reinforcement and runaway Negroes that had to sustain the battle in a retreating fight. They were earnestly fighting to check the whites until the town women and children could hide some of their stuff and make their escape. A runner came to them and told them they were about to be surrounded by a squadron of horsemen and foot soldiers who were trying to close their lines on the rear of the town. They all quickly retreated, some to save themselves, others their horses, to try to escape at an open space of ground where the lines were not yet closed. The Indians and Negroes, being mostly afoot, saved themselves by swimming over the river. John Moniac and two others went through before the lines were closed.

Weatherford and McPherson, on horses, viewed the lines to see if there was any gap that would permit their escape; but they found it all closed. They were unable to fight, but they preferred death to surrender or being prisoners to an army. The only avenue left for them to escape was to leap off a bluff, between fifty and sixty feet high, at the junction of the creek and river. Weatherford was mounted on the swift and mettlesome courser Abbanonair, who in part belonged to Benjamin Baldwin of Macon County. Weatherford knew the horse's mettle and docile disposition to the will of the rider and that he would not fly aside from any direction given him, especially if urged by the spur.

Weatherford proposed taking the first leap from the bluff. He rode his horse up to the margin and let him see it, then reined him nearly thirty yards, rifle in hand, then struck off for the bluff, and touched the horse with the spur. The generous beast leaped off as though he meant to reach the opposite shore. Weatherford said he seemed to go straight forward for more than thirty feet, then turned nearly head down and kept a curving flight until he struck the water. Man and horse separated long before they touched the water; then they swam ashore together, gun and all unhurt. When he reached the shore Weatherford saw his flight repeated by McPherson. He said it was awfully curious to see a man and horse fly through the air like a cormorant or fish eagle when he pounces on a fish.[92] Both got to shore unhurt and with their friends who swam the river bore the news of the destruction of Holy Ground town wherever they went.

In the conflict with General Claiborne the hostiles supposed that they lost about thirty men, that is, about twenty warriors and seven runaway Negroes who had joined the Indians with the expectation of being free. Their freedom would come about when the Negroes and the Indians would conquer and destroy the white people, according to the say of the prophets.

A few days after the fight, Francis and his men returned to see about their dead and get the household stuff they had buried. Instead of their houses they found only smoke and ashes.

The burning of Ekon-achaka gave relief to the white people of the settlements downriver; it finally closed the hostile operations of the lower-town Indians, the parties of Josiah Francis and Paddy Walsh. The latter moved to the Othlewallee camps again. There they had to organize their force as they expected an immediate attack from Georgia or Mississippi or perhaps from both places at once.

Josiah Francis

I have taken an historical view of Josiah Francis from the time of his becoming a prophet to this period. I shall here tell the events of his later life. . . . Francis, whose father was a resident of Coosawda for many years, was, it is said, a blacksmith of French parents who were very superstitious. Francis's parents raised him as an Indian and in Indian superstitious ideas, so it was not a great change for him to admire Tecumseh's pretense of knowing future events. But Francis was of a timid nature; the burning of the Holy Ground so alarmed him that he had no time to think of prophesying in serious terms of mischief. In his terror and the incertitude of events his thoughts were of how he and his few adherents could escape to Pensacola for security out of a storm that he could see without revelation—the overturn of the nation and its customs. He and his party moved to Pensacola where he influenced the Indians to join Major Nicholl, who then commanded the British force at that station. Francis attended Captain Woodbine in the attack of Mobile Point. Then he returned to Pensacola and stayed there until after the failure of the British at New Orleans, when he was carried to England by Major Nicholl with the promise of being well received by the King or his ministers for his indefatigable exertions in influencing the hostile tribes in favor of England.

On his departure for Europe, Francis directed his family to await his return by living among the Seminoles. He was accompanied by a Coosawda chief called Moulton. They returned with two men named Ambrister and Arbuthnot and began to give the Seminoles friendly English talks. Later, by mistake, they went aboard an American gunboat, where they were arrested. By an order of General Jackson they ended their eventful lives by being hung on the yardarm of the gunboat.[93]

Francis was a man of no talent, very still and reserved in his manners in the ordinary scenes of life. He was of no turn to command respect or esteem, but undoubtedly by his fanatical pretensions to knowledge of future things he overbalanced all sober reason in his tribe, which led to their wild and thoughtless outbreaking. So he became one of a few who caused the downfall of the Ispocoga tribes.

Creek Towns Regroup

I must apologize to the reader for digressing by narrating the fall of the Holy Ground town before the battle of Autossee, which preceded the former by a month. But I did this because I was treating Josiah Francis's transactions. So I shall go back nearly two months.

From the time that General Jackson entered the Creek

nation and destroyed the Littasuck and Tallasseehatchee and discomfited the largest armament that Littasuck ever embodied, the hostiles had begun to be more cautious and to think how they might evade a total annihilation of their nation, and to pay more attention to their scattered dwellings and move them so as to make their situations more dense and to better their concerns of war. They had seen the impropriety of having a war at the door of every town and the repelling of the foe to be done alone by the warriors of each town that was attacked. They saw that even their largest towns would be inevitably overthrown when brought singly into contact with a well equipped army of white people, that their small towns in their present local situations would fall one by one and be an easy prey to the invader, until the nation would be consumed piecemeal. So the conclusion in the debating councils of their prophets and head warriors was that certain towns should be selected and different bodies at particular places of natural strength should be formed; those different stations or encampments would be strong enough to contend with and repel any invading army that might attack them.

They pitched on the Othlewallee (or Cluwallee) and the Autossee as convenient places, where they were in the habit of organizing war parties and dispensing provisions. These two stations on the Tallapoosa were for all townsmen from the Tallassee to Wetumpka and as far down the river as the bend below the city of Montgomery to resort to for safety in case of an enemy incursion. The Autossee station was the most respectable in numbers of men, about a thousand warriors. Othlewallee at all times had more than five hundred men.

Both stations looked on Paddy Walsh as their prophetic commander, although he principally resided at the Cluwallee camps. Even before the fall of the two Autossee towns both camps had kept their swift runners on the lookout toward Talladega and Hillabee. They had no idea of any other enemy being out but the Tennesseans, whose army they had expected to have to fight for over a month. They got the news continually from runaway Negroes that great preparation was being made, in men and provisions, in Mississippi and Georgia for an invasion. But the invasion would not transpire until towards the spring of the ensuing year. They had not heard for some time, for certain, of the movements of the Tennessee troops, only that they were in the Creek nation. The Indian view of all this was that the pretense of inaction was to lull them into inattention and inaction. They believed that the white people intended to press on them all at once and crush them with an overwhelming force. The Tennessee troops, they thought, were quiet only until they could get a recruit of men or provisions to commence, and that the first movement would be a signal for a general invasion. If, as they contemplated, this was so, they were determined to meet the foe despite all hazards and take death if so ordained, for a man could die but once.

Attack on Autossee Towns

So when the two Autossee towns were attacked by General Floyd, the Cluwallees expected an immediate brush with the Georgians or Tennesseans. They said they had been and still were in hourly expectation of such an event. After they had held their meeting, and all things remained quiet and still, Coosa Micco, the commander and head of the Autossee town, sent for his confidante and intimate friend, a Cluwallee called Te-wa-sub-buk-le, who was one of the principal prophets and the chief in command of his townsmen. Coosa Micco wanted to consult him on the propriety of defensive or operative measures, which of the two had best be pursued. These two men were still in deep and private conversation about three or four hours before day when a man, who had camped out for an early turkey hunt, came running into the town and announced the near approach of a large army of white people.

As the Indians had long expected it, they were not dismayed or surprised. There was an instant order for the infirm old men to cross the river with the women, children, and Negroes and disperse them into places of safety below the Othlewallee camp. If they succeeded in repelling the foe, of which they had no doubt, they would send word to return. The aforesaid matters being hastily arranged, Te-wa-sub-buk-le proposed that Coosa Micco keep the command of the upper Autossee town near the mouth of Calabee Creek, where the Tallassees, under the McQueens,[94] and the Autossees were stationed. Coosa Micco, according to the prophet, must await the onset of the enemy in the front edge of the town; and he, Te-wa-sub-buk-ke, would go down to the other part of town, where there were warriors from minor towns out of the fork between the two rivers. The prophet intended to direct the action himself and await the enemy's onset in the borders of the town. They had scarcely time to make known to each other the hasty plans of disposing their men to meet the enemy when the runner announced that the enemy had appeared in the wood bordering the town.

The anxiously expecting Indians awaited the attack, which came at daylight.[95] Coosa Micco, glad for action, saw the army of white people moving forward and begin to attack with small arms and cannon. He called his men to arrange themselves properly and meet the enemy. He returned their salute and accompanied it with a general war whoop. He encouraged his men to fight bravely and calmly without shrinking back and not to waste their fire in fear. He tried to infuse in them his spirit of fighting, both by words and actions.

While Coosa Micco was encouraging and exhorting his men, news was brought to him that Te-wa-sub-buk-le, the prophet, was killed and that the warriors were giving ground rapidly. On hearing this, Coosa Micco mounted his horse and sped to the lower-town warriors to try to repair the damage. But the cause was scarcely retrievable; the greater part of them were retreating, making for the ponds of water by their houses. They were in a panic after they had been charged by the horsemen. Coosa Micco rallied and stopped some of them; he saw that they were not willing to fight front to front. So he thought to turn to the left rear flank of the American troop, hoping to cause the warriors to rally and fight. In trying to turn their flank, he said, he saw that the enemy would always present a solid front. By the time he reached the uppermost level (thlaw-a-nubba) he began to see his own horsemen mix together in mortal strife. They gave ground and chased themselves into the big reed brake. This convinced him that he was whipped and overcome. He himself was badly wounded in two places from bullets, and chopped across the cheek by a sword, and his horse shot through the neck and body. Being very faint from loss of blood, Coosa Micco dismounted at length and went into the reed brake and gave up the Autossee town to the conquerors.

Before the commencement of the battle, Coosa Micco and Te-wa-sub-buk-le had sent a pressing word to the Cluwallee camps that they were about to be attacked and to come to their assistance. But the Cluwallees never came or so much as started. Why Paddy Walsh never came to their assistance I could never ascertain.

In the Autossee battle the hostiles supposed that they lost probably eighty men and more than a hundred wounded.

Their complete defeat, and the burning of their town, broke up the hostile settlement in the Autossees. It gave them a complete scare and set them to rambling. Many of them took up quarters in the Othlewallee camps. Some made their way with their families to inaccessible places in the swamps or the forest, and others went to Pensacola for safety among the Spaniards.

The hostile camps by this time began to feel the want of ammunition. A general meeting was called by the hostile chiefs and prophets to view their situation.

They sent for William Weatherford to attend. He had confined himself to his home ever since the affair of Talladega Fort. When he received their request he went to the Cluwallee camps.

The prophets Paddy and High-headed Jim mentioned the alarming state of their affairs, through the scarcity of powder and lead; on a strict examination they had made for these articles among the warriors, [they concluded] they could not stand another battle such as Autossee. Because Weatherford had assisted High-headed Jim (whom the Indians called Cusseta Haijo) on a former occasion of their hostilities and had succeeded in getting a supply of powder and lead from the authorities of Spain, they all deemed Weatherford as the man best qualified to go to Pensacola with a sufficient escort to ensure him safety back with the powder and lead. So it was agreed, according to the wish of the prophetic authorities, High-headed Jim being one of the prophets.

The day appointed to start, they took an escort of 390 mounted men and pursued their way to Pensacola to see their good friend the Spanish governor. On their arrival in that metropolis in pursuance of the mission from the hostile authorities, they demanded an audience with his excellency. In their tete-a-tete they pleased his excellency so well that he made them a present of three horseloads of powder and lead, with which they returned to the Cluwallee camps. The drooping spirits of that section of the hostile party were lifted and they revived their neglected war dances, because once more they had plenty of powder and lead.

Battle of Calabee

In the midst of their joy and festivities (their envoys had scarcely got rested from their long and troublesome missionary journey) it was announced by one of their swift runners that he had seen a large army of Georgians on the march with cannon in their train marching along the Georgia road. On this news Paddy immediately sent swift runners to all persons, places of encampment, and towns for the warriors to rendezvous at the Othlewallee camps. The warriors all attended to the words promptly.

When they had all assembled, they were informed by the prophet that the white men were forming a camp on the level of Chuseekna Wockna,[96] which is "the spike horn bucks bed." It was their business and interest to fight and dislodge them before they made their camp too strong. In the evening the whole force marched to the west shore of Calabee about a mile from the American camp.

The Indians numbered 1,274 warriors, stripped and painted red, all in readiness to give the camp of the enemy a night encounter. Then the question was proposed by the chiefs and leaders of the townsmen: in what manner was the action to be conducted? The plan of attack was left by the chiefs and prophets to four men: the leading prophet, Paddy Walsh; McGillivray;[97] Weatherford; and High-headed Jim. Paddy gave his opinion first of all: the warriors were to be ready and near at hand to the American camp and attack the whites as they were going to sleep. Their attack would be against two squares of the camp; the attack would be close and severe. If they made an impression against the enemy's camp by daylight, they would keep up the fight; but if by dawn they made no perceptible impression on the enemy, Paddy said they would break off in a retreat and quit the fight.

Paddy's plan was sanctioned only by High-headed Jim. McGillivray and Weatherford dissented from Paddy's plan, saying that it seemed to them that Paddy's proposed manner for the fight was only to encounter the enemy saying, "I am to be defeated in the end." A man could not fight hard with a limit on himself, to run off at a set time. For their part they would fight as long as they could see any chance; they wanted no limitations in their battle.

Weatherford said that he would propose his idea of a plan. He proposed to begin at the same time of night. The white people's fashion of camping was for all the commanding officers to take their place in the center of the camp square. Weatherford's opinion was that Paddy take three hundred men or more, rifle and tomahawk in hand, and move up slyly to one of the squares, raise the scream, and make an opening through it with the tomahawk. At the same time the rest of the red-painted men would make a charging attack on two other squares. While this was operating, and in the confusion that must ensue, the three hundred men in the first square would endeavor to kill all the officers and fight their way out at the same square. As it was the manner of the white people to fight as they were directed by their officers, a great confusion must follow without anyone to give necessary orders. On the loss of their officers, the confusion would give the assailants of the two squares a chance of destructively penetrating the squares at the same time. The three hundred men when out of the alignment would keep the line they first penetrated. Eventually the common soldiers, not knowing what do do, would run from their camp for the woods and home.

The two prophets replied to Weatherford in an authoritative and prophetic manner; they seemed to shudder at some hidden motive in what he proposed, as they would at a contagious pestilence. At length they said that his plan was a measure of insanity and desperation, a sure and unnecessary sacrifice of three hundred men. Paddy said that it seemed to him that Weatherford and McGillivray wished to jeopardize his life and that they were

Tustennuggee Emathla, known as High-headed Jim, or Jim Boy, was chief of the Autossees and led the Indian attack at the Battle of Burnt Corn. This portrait was painted by Charles Bird King in the 1820s, when a Creek delegation came to Washington, D.C. on tribal business.
(Photograph courtesy of SMITHSONIAN INSTITUTION, BUREAU OF AMERICAN ETHNOLOGY*)*

trying publicly to force him to take command of and attempt a measure that would destroy him and many others—a measure that neither of them dared undertake.

At this insinuation and public questioning of their prowess and courage, Weatherford and McGillivray jumped to their feet and said that one or both of them was willing to lead the painted men and perform the action or die in the attempt. . . . They said they were convinced that man is born to die and that he could lose his life but once. They remarked that they would prefer death to a fearful neglect of duty to their country and its liberties.

Then there was a call made for that number of red-painted men. But very few offered themselves for the attack, because they knew the prophet had spoken against the measure as if by inspiration. Weatherford took their neglect of his advice and offer of service as a public insult.

His high ideas of honor did not allow him to fight following Paddy's plan after publicly arguing against it. So he told Paddy it was his intention to go home, leaving him to fight his cautious half-fights if he was determined to do so. Weatherford and his friends mounted their horses and made for home that same night.[98]

Left to follow the dictates of his own mind, Paddy Walsh conducted his men across Calabee Creek and assaulted the Georgia army according to his plan. In the morning, after the night's encounter, he was severely wracked with loss. In the battle forty warriors were killed; as to the wounded, they could not guess the number. One man of importance was lost; it was High-headed Jim, or Cusseta. He was one of their greatest warriors and principal prophets.

William McGillivray, though highly insulted by the prophets that evening in the debate, nevertheless laid all irritations of mind aside and accompanied Paddy in order to be with and bear his part with his townsmen in the battle. He participated in the defeat and the hard race for an escape from the battleground in the morning. Paddy made his escape that fatal morning, although he was badly wounded.

The defeat at Calabee was fatal to the hostiles. It closed the hostile operations of the lower towns and finally broke up the unity of the hostiles and their ability to organize for hostile purposes. The defeat silenced the old and new war dance and whoop of many of their most conspicuous warriors. None of the lower-town chiefs ever entered the battlefield after the Calabee affair; they appeared to be paralyzed and inattentive to national affairs.[99]

The chiefs mostly spent their time carelessly inactive.

There were a few indigent ones who were innately prone to mischief. They occasionally made excursions down the river into the settlements of the white people, where they were interested enough to kill the owner in order to get his plunder and horse; and in a few instances they killed whole families and plundered and burned houses. These marauding parties confined themselves in their excursions principally to Monroe and Clarke Counties. The lower towns appeared to feel spite toward the people of that department more than any other, and kept up their hostilities until the Horseshoe Bend was taken and the last of their forces destroyed by General Jackson.

When the hostile party heard that Menewa, or Kelisennehaw, had at length agreed to his towns painting for the war and painted himself likewise, they were elated, always having had an exalted opinion of his skill and prowess in Indian warfare. But when they heard that after his many conflicts with the Tennessee army he was destroyed, with his fortification, at the Horseshoe, they sunk in their opinion of themselves. . . . The whole posse of them appeared desirous to get out of the reach of harm and to live neutrally and on neutral grounds. Their retributive spirit of retaliation and war was broken. . . . Their dejection made them seek shelter in other places and quit their home and nation where they were fearful hourly of having to encounter a powerful and fortunate enemy, a foe that they had often tried to overcome and could not withstand. The Ispocoga, or Creek, tribe could not in their national home find ease of mind. . . . They made their way to Pensacola in Spanish Florida to get shelter and a little respite from the apprehensions of dire destruction.

Paddy Walsh

While I am treating of lower towns and their exit, I think it would not be taken amiss in me by the reader to try an exposition of the transactions of Paddy's latter days to the gallows.

James Walsh, the father of Paddy, was a South Carolinian. In the American Revolution he was a despicable, murdering swamp Tory, which caused him after the close of that contest to leave the area where he had perpetrated so many crimes. He settled in the Creek nation, where he became the father of Paddy. Paddy lost his father while very young, so of course he was raised as other Alabama Indians are, in a state of nature, without knowing the restraints of mind. Paddy was under the ordinary size of men, his stature not exceeding five feet and two or three inches. The hair on his head came very low on his forehead, and he had a wide mouth which made him look almost inhumanly ugly. He was a great Indian linguist, speaking the Creek, Alabama, Chickasaw, and Choctaw languages fluently. He was a great natural orator, both persuasive and commanding. He was so deep in his manner of reasoning, and gifted with such eloquence, that no Indian could withstand him on any point.

He was a brave man, known to shrink from daring action but once: when he refused to enter General Floyd's lines at the Calabee battle. He told his Alabama people that the Indians were unable to fight the white people with any success, therefore it was his opinion that they had better go to Pensacola and be out of the way of harm until the Creek nation could effect a peace. For his own part, as he was wounded and it would take some time and doctoring to cure him, he thought it best to go the river with his relatives in their canoes and go up some canebrake creek where they could not be found until he got well. After he got well, as it had become a principle in him to hate the white people, it was his wish to be in feud with them so long as he lived. He never would miss a chance to destroy one of them. So he and his relatives ensconced themselves in the canebrakes. Later he moved down the river, to a place called Standing Peach Tree, where he was stationed nearly a year.

One day, when Paddy and five or six of his men were sauntering on a sand shoal, they saw a boat coming down the river with seven men on board. From their caps, they appeared to be of the army. The Indians went up on the bank of the river for fear of being seen. When the boat neared the sand bank, the soldiers turned it to land; they got out and made for some shade trees near where the Indians hid. Just as the soldiers began to eat, the Indians fired on them and killed three of them. [In the ensuing fight] all but one of the soldiers was killed. The Indians took the survivor a prisoner and kept him with them nearly two months, before he cut his own throat. The officer who had been killed in the encounter was named Wilcox.[100] The prisoner told the Indians he was a lieutenant, sent on business to Fort Claiborne and that his regiment lay at Fort Jackson.

After this incident Paddy moved to the west side of the river and lay in the canebrakes concealed for some time before he attempted anything (he said he would retaliate on the white people for what they had done to his people). It got noised about that the Indians were in large numbers near the lower Standing Peach Tree. A party of whites organized in Clarke County went to kill the Indians. In the Indian camp they killed Paddy's aunt. In retaliation for the murder, Paddy killed two men, Joseph Foster and Joseph Milstead, and broke up the new settlement. Then General Gaines sent a Lieutenant Nelson with a command of men who got hold of the Dog Warrior, who betrayed Paddy into his hands. Nelson carried Paddy to Fort Claiborne, with a young Indian, to be kept by the military until he could be tried for his notorious deeds. In about six weeks Paddy and his companion made their escape from the guard. But fearing the consequences of his escape, the Indians gave him up again. At Claiborne he was tried for the murders he had committed and convicted of crimes without any evidence for or against him. A lying interpreter, who gave false answers to the court, said that Paddy acknowledged the deed, gave himself great credit for it, and vowed it was no more than he intended doing again. He was found guilty and hanged at Fort Claiborne.

Though he was small, ugly, and a diminutive man in personal appearance, he was the greatest prophetic warrior that the Ispocoga, or Creek, tribe ever had. . . . If he had been more pacific in his disposition toward the U. S., he could have turned the scale of war to peace and saved the great effusion of blood, which he was the cause of through his wicked prophecies.

Now, as I have carried the lower towns to the dispersion of their nation, I shall fall back two or three months and revive the history of the upper towns of the Coosa and Tallapoosa in their different attitudes and collision in war.[101]

Wyman's Notes
with editor's notes in brackets

1. National legends of the Choctaw-Muscogee tribes which have been handed down in several forms indicate that the Muscogee or Creek Indians moved in very ancient times from their primeval homes west of the Mississippi River to the country between the Coosa and the Savannah. For variant forms of the tradition see Louis Le Clerc Milford, *Memoire ou coup-d'oeil rapide sur mes differens voyages et mon sejour dans la nation Creck*, p. 229; *Missionary Herald* 24:215; Henry Rowe Schoolcraft, *Historical and Statistical Information Respecting the History, Conditions, and Prospects of the Indian Tribes of the United States*, vol. I, p. 300; Benjamin Hawkins, *A Sketch of the Creek Country*, p. 81; Daniel G. Brinton, "National Legend of the Chahta-Muskokee Tribes," *American Historical Magazine*, February 1870, p. 7. This last named is an exceedingly interesting document. Brinton, the learned and careful student of American antiquities, found this legend in a work published by Samuel Urlsperger at Halle in 1741, entitled *von Reck's Diarum von seiner Reise nach Georgian im Gahr 1735*, and translated it

for the *American Historical Magazine*. Brinton's translation is the basis of Albert S. Gatschet's valuable work *A Migration Legend of the Creek Indians*.

2. A very old name of the Muscogee tribe. *Is-po-ko-ke* is the correct form of the word. It seems to be the plural form of Ispoke, a Creek word meaning "the end" or "the last." The meaning of Ispokoke then is "the end people." Mary E. W. Robertson, a highly cultivated lady, who has for many years lived among the Creeks as a missionary of the Presbyterian Church, translates it "world's end people." This seems to point the claim of the Muscogees that they were the first inhabitants of this region. Ispokoke is an ancient name of the Tuckabatchee town of the Creeks. Hawkins, p. 27. The white traders' corrupt form of the name is "Spoke Oak." There were many Ispokoke miccos or chiefs throughout the towns.
3. The etymology and meaning of *Muscogee* (properly spelled, as pronounced, *Maskoke*), which is the general tribal name of the Creeks, has never been satisfactorily determined. The Creeks say that the meaning of the word was lost many generations ago. For various conjectures, see Gatschet, p. 53.
4. There may be some foundation of truth in this tradition. In a sketch of the history of the Creek Indians, which their great chieftain, General Alexander McGillivray, wrote for General Henry Knox in 1790, it is said that the first homes of the Alabamas were in the Tensaw region of Alabama. McGillivray's sketch is incomplete. I found the fragment some years ago among the Knox papers deposited in the library of the Massachusetts Historic-Genealogical Society of Boston.

The copy which I made at the time is hid away somewhere among my miscellaneous collections, and cannot just now be found. I refer to it from memory alone. It is certain, nevertheless, that there were some towns of the Alabamas at the head of the Alabama River, above and below the site of Montgomery, as far back in the past as 1540, when De Soto passed through this country. The chroniclers of De Soto's expedition mention several towns in this quarter that certainly bear Alabama names: Ullibahali, which means in the Alabama dialect, "mulberry people"; Tascalusa, which means "black warrior"; and Toasi (Towassa), of which the meaning is unknown to me. Two hundred and fifty years later there was a town of the Alabamas called Towassa situated on the left bank of the Alabama River, four miles below the present Montgomery. Long after the inhabitants were removed, the bluff on which the town stood and the steamboat landing hard by were called by the whites Towassa.

The French historians of Louisiana tell of a band of Touachas, who in 1705 fled for refuge from the Spanish settlements in Florida to Mobile in order to escape the constant assaults of the Alabamas. They were settled on Mobile River, a few miles below Fort Louis. It is hard to tell where this small tribe lived before they came to the French—perhaps on the Appalachicola River. Surely they were a different people from the Towassees of the upper Alabama. Gatschet thinks they were the same. Andre Penicaut, "Relation," in Pierre Margry's *Decouvertes et Etablissements des Francais dans l'Ouest et dans le Sud de l'Amerique Septentrionale*, vol. V, pp. 457, 486; Bernard de La Harpe, *Journal Historique de l'establissement des Francais a la Louisiana*, pp. 101, 103; Gatschet, p. 110.

5. The Autauga town was just below the mouth of Autauga Creek on the right bank of the river. The whites afterwards built a town on the same bluff, which was named Washington. On account of the insalubrity of the situation, Washington was abandoned some thirty years ago, and is now one of the "dead towns" of Alabama. The name Autauga is pure Muscogee and means "the people down the river." This town was so named by the Creeks because it was the last town passed by one going down the river from the junction. Properly spelled as the Indians pronounced it, it is Ah-tah-ke, which is the plural form of Ah-tah, "down-stream." Hawkins spells it Au-tau-gee.
6. Literally, Oche-ap-ofa, which means "among the hickory trees." The white traders and Indian countrymen called it "The Hickory Ground." It was situated in the fork of the Coosa and Tallapoosa Rivers about one mile below the present city of Wetumpka. It bore the name of Oche-ap-ofa long before 1813.
7. This is the plural form of Chel-o-kee, which is the Creek word for Cherokee. As the Cherokees differed radically in language and stock from the Muscogees, the name Che-lok-ulke was applied by the Creeks probably to other neighboring tribes speaking a foreign tongue.
8. On the oldest French maps the Alabama River is called Coussa. I conjecture that the name Alabama was first given to it by the French after they built Fort Toulouse in 1717. Yet it is certain that in Tristan de Luna's time

(1559) it was sometimes called Olibahali or Ullibali, which is pretty close to the French form, Alibamons or Alibamo. Andres Gonzalez de Barcia Carballido y Zuniga, *Ensayo cronologico para la historia general de la Florida*, p. 34. "El rio mas grande que por alli avia se llamava Olibahali." Fray Agustin Davila Padilla, *Historia de la Fundacion y Discurso de la Provincia de Santiago de Mexico*, p. 202.

9. According to a tradition given orally by Sekopecke, a very old Indian of the Alabama tribe, to D. W. Eakin in 1847, the Alabamas sprang out of the ground between the Cahawba and Alabama Rivers. Schoolcraft, vol. I, p. 266. Milford gives a confused account of their long wandering eastward from their early home on Red River after the conquest of Mexico by Cortez, until they were finally settled in union with Creeks on the Alabama. Milford, p. 236. Albert James Pickett (*History of Alabama and Incidentally of Georgia and Mississippi, from the Earliest Period*, vol. I, p. 78) follows Milford without seeming to suspect any sophistication.

   [Another origin myth, told to John R. Swanton in the 1920s, says the Alabamas came out of the earth where the Alabama and Tombigbee Rivers flow together. An owl hooted and scared most of the people back into the ground, making them few in number. John R. Swanton, *Early History of the Creek Indians and Their Neighbors*, Bureau of American Ethnology Bulletin, no. 73 (Washington, D.C., 1922), p. 192.]

10. That the Alabamas were builders of mounds on the Alabama River may safely be conjectured. We know of one mound at least constructed by them within the his-

toric period. In 1899 Clarence B. Moore of Philadelphia dug down the ancient mound at the Charlotte Thompson place on the left bank of the Alabama River six miles below Montgomery. This mound is at or near the site of the old Alabama town of Pauwokte. Moore found mingled indiscriminately throughout this mound, from top to bottom, implements and ornaments both of Indian and European workmanship, thus proving that this mound was built after these Indians had become acquainted with Europeans—perhaps with De Soto's men. Clarence B. Moore, "Certain Aboriginal Remains of the Alabama River," *Journal of the Academy of Natural Sciences of Philadelphia* 11 (1899):289-337.

11. The Coosawda (Ko-a-sah-te, Ko-a-shah-te, Ko-shatta, Ku-shatte) town was on a high red bluff on the Alabama a little below the point where the Louisville and Nashville Railroad bridge crosses the river a few miles above Montgomery. A town of white people was established on the spot about 1817 and flourished for some twenty years or more. It has long since disappeared. Mary E. W. Robertson informs me that "the Cusahties are only a town or band of the Alabamas." They and the Alabamas are "people of one fire." An educated gentleman of the Creek nation, Indian Territory, Ward Crachman, who is of the Alabama tribe, informs me that the name Ku-ah-sah-te is of Muscogee and not of Alabama origin. It is only the Alabama variation of the favorite Creek name Ekon-chatte, which means "the red bluff."

The Indian town of Coosawda was burned in April 1814 by Colonel John H. Gibson of General Jackson's command. Peter J. Hamilton and Thomas M. Owen, eds., "Tatum's Journal," in *Transactions of the Alabama Historical Society*, II, p. 134.

12. Stiggins seems to know nothing of the custom, peculiar to the Alabamas, of celebrating the ripening of the mulberries by a solemn religious festival. Let it be remembered that Ullibahali means in the Alabama tongue "the mulberry people." James Adair, *The History of the American Indians*, p. 267; William Marinus Willet, *A Narrative of the Military Actions of Colonel Marinus Willett*, p. 37.

    [Stiggins, raised for the most part in the white man's world, shows little understanding of the Indians' belief system. For an excellent discussion of how southern Indians worshipped, see Charles Hudson, *The Southeastern Indians* (Knoxville: University of Tennessee Press, 1976), pp. 120-83. Hudson is considered the foremost authority on southeastern Indians.]

13. There was an earlier removal of a band of the Alabamas to the west of the Mississippi in 1763, under the leadership of an old medal chief named Tamathle Mingo. Jean-Bernard Bossu, *Nouveaux voyages dans l'Amerique Septentrionale*, p. 133; William Bartram, *Travels Through North and South Carolina, Georgia, East and West Florida*, p. 427. See also Peter J. Hamilton's *Colonial Mobile*, p. 183.

    [Today around one thousand Alabama-Koasatis live in a settlement in the Big Thicket area of southeast Texas where they have built a cultural heritage center. Virginia Pounds Brown and Laurella Owens, *The World of the Southern Indians* (Birmingham, Ala.: Beechwood Books, 1983), p. 131.]

14. "The original seats of the Uchees were east of the Coosa and probably of the Chattahoochee and they consider themselves the most ancient inhabitants of the country. It appears certain that at the beginning of the eighteenth century, they were, at least in part, seated on the western banks of the Savannah." Albert Gallatin, *A Synopsis of the Indian Tribes Within the United States East of the Rocky Mountains*. Hawkins says they were formerly settled in small villages on both sides of the Savannah (p.61). See also Wright's *Life of Oglethorpe*, p. 215.

The principal town of the Uchees in Hawkins's time and afterwards was on the Alabama side of the Chattahoochee River below the mouth of Uchee Creek.

15. Stiggins paints the Uchees in colors quite too dark. Hawkins, on the contrary, speaks well of them (p. 62): "These people are more civil and orderly than their neighbors; their women are more chaste, and their men better hunters. They are industrious, compared with their neighbors; the men take part in the labors of the women, and are more constant in their attachment to their women than is usual among red people."

16. No tribal or linguistic connection between the Uchees and any other nation has ever been traced. They stand alone and aloof among the American tribes like the "mysterious Etruscans" among the nations of ancient Italy.

[Descendants of the Uchees, who moved to the west with the Creeks in 1829 and 1836, meet annually in Columbus, Georgia, for a tribal celebration. Brown and Owens, p. 135.]

17. The Puccun-tallahassee town was on Hatchet Creek in the present Coosa County. The council house of the town was, in 1834, on the south side of the creek about three miles from the Coosa River. The name is pure Muscogee, being compounded of Pakana, "apple," "peach," "plum," and Tallahassee, "old town." Hawkins translates it, "May-Apple Old Town." There is no tradition save the one mentioned in the text that these Indians were anciently of alien stock. Bossu, Bernard Romans, and others name them as one of the Creek tribes.

18. According to Chekilli's version of the national legend delivered to Governor Oglethorpe in 1735, the Abekah was one of the four tribes that came from the west in prehistoric times and settled on the rivers of Alabama and Georgia. The four tribes were the Abekah, Cussetah, Chickasaw, and Alibamo. They found the Coosas already seated on Coosa River. Brinton, p. 8; Gatschet, p. 248.

According to Tussekiah Micco's version delivered to Colonel Hawkins about the year 1800, three tribes, the Cussetah, Cowetah, and Chickasuh, came eastwardly together and found the Abekah at Coosa River. Hawkins, p. 82.

19. The fact here mentioned is important in determining the linguistic kinship of the Abekas. The distinctive form of the affirmative particle may be regarded as characteristic. Stiggins thinks that the Abekas were pure Muscogee. Yet the Abeka word of assent—"aw," as he writes it—indicates that their dialect was Choctaw rather than Muscogee, for the affirmative particle

in Muscogee, expressing assent or approval, is *kah*—a foreshortening by phonetic decay of the Muscogee *hinkah*, which means "yes." In Choctaw, on the other hand, assent is expressed by the emphatic monosyllable *yaw*, which is about the same as the Abeka *aw*. The distinction runs parallel with the difference between the langue d'oc and the langue d'oil of the old French.

20. 1540.

[Even though his date is incorrect, Stiggins must have had access to information about the De Soto expedition. The only clue as to possible sources appears in Albert James Pickett's Preface to his *History of Alabama and Incidentally of Georgia and Mississippi, from the Earliest Period*, 2 vols. (Charleston: Walker and James, 1851). Pickett follows the statement that he briefly examined the Stiggins manuscript by saying, "Stiggins received some particulars of the route of De Soto during his boyhood from the lips of the oldest Indians" (pp. 11-12). Pickett also writes that much of his own information about De Soto came from the statements of Alexander McGillivray, a kinsman by marriage of Stiggins. Pickett's other sources may well have been available to Stiggins also. Though not a scholar, Stiggins was fairly well educated for his day.]

21. No mention is made in any of the De Soto chronicles of either Nickajack or Coosa-wattee.
22. There was a town in the Talladega country, in De Soto's time, called Talla-muchassee, which is pure Creek for "new town"; but no mention is made of Coosa Tulmuchessee. *Narrative of the Gentleman of Elvas*, XVII.
23. The Abekoochee town was on the north side of Tal-

lasseehatchee Creek five miles from the Coosa River. The old Coosa town which Stiggins calls Coosa Tulmuchessee occupied a high plateau on the left bank of the Coosa River between Talladega and Tallasseehatchee Creeks.

It is certain that the Coosas spoke a dialect of Choctaw. It is highly probable that the Abekas, Abekoochees, and Coosas were "people of one fire," and all of Choctaw lineage and speech.

24. De Soto, so far as we know, built no fortifications in this quarter. The remains of the old fort near the Abekoochee town was visited and described by Major Caleb Swan in 1790. Schoolcraft, vol. V, p. 283. The Reverend Hosea Holcombe saw it in 1829: "supposed to be the ruins of an ancient Town-house." *History of the Baptists in Alabama*, p. 219.

[Since De Soto was seeking gold, Abekoochee was a likely spot for encampment. In 1853 geologist Tuomey found gold mines in operation at Abekoochee, which at one time employed six hundred men. Michael Tuomey, Second Biennial Report on the Geology of Alabama (Montgomery, 1858).]

25. [Swanton has this to say about the drums: "Nevertheless from what Swan says regarding the number of British drums in Creek towns and the esteem in which they were held it is possible that the Abihka specimen was of much more recent introduction. See Schoolcraft, Ind. Tribes, v, p. 275" (p. 252).]

26. Stiggins was wrong as to the situation of Mabila.

[The location of Mabila continues to confound historians. In 1987 the Alabama De Soto Commission defined Soto's route to be north of the path set by the

1939 De Soto Commission. It placed Mabila near Selma, whereas the 1939 commission believed it to be in Clarke County. Archeological digs have failed to turn up evidence from either location. John C. Hall, "The Search for Hernando De Soto," *Alabama Heritage*, Spring 1987, no. 4, pp. 12-27.]

27. The town of Hothlewallee, called by the whites Cluwalle, Clewalle, Kewally, etc., was on the north side of the Tallapoosa River, nearly opposite the mouth of Line (Okfuskee) Creek. Hawkins speaks of "the remains of a ditch, which surrounded a fortification," in this vicinity. Perhaps this is the "vieux fort Toulouse," laid down on some old French maps.

[Owen says Hoithlewalli, a very ancient town, had the privilege of declaring war. The declaration was first forwarded to Tuckabatchee and thence to other towns. This town was visited by De Soto August 31, 1540, and twenty years later by the Tristan de Luna expedition. The town was destroyed in the Creek War; the inhabitants fled to the Spanish in Pensacola. Thomas McAdory Owen, *History of Alabama and Dictionary of Alabama Biography*, 4 vols. (Chicago: S. J. Clarke Publishing Co., 1921), pp. 696-97.]

28. After the destruction of the Natchez by the French in 1729, a remnant of the tribe was hospitably received by the Creeks, and settled on Tallasseehatchee Creek. The Natchez town was five miles above Abekoochee. Their native tongue is still spoken by the Natchez who live among the Creeks in the Indian Territory.

29. "Busk" is the white man's name for the Posketa, or Green Corn festival, described hereinafter.

30. "There is a very large cave north of the town [Ahbekooche], the entrance of which is small on the side of a hill. It is much divided, and some of the rooms appear as the work of art." Hawkins, p. 41.

[Located near Childersburg, Alabama, and known today as De Soto Caverns, the cave is open to the public. Local lore says that Wright, an Indian trader from South Carolina, was killed by the Creeks, angry at the whites' desecration of that sacred place. Virginia Van der Veer Hamilton, *Seeing Historic Alabama: Fifteen Guided Tours* (University: University of Alabama Press, 1982), p. 107.]

31. [Swanton says that in the Natchez language this probably means a "very old person" (p. 316).]
32. In the early part of the eighteenth century there were Shawano [Shawnee] towns on the Savannah River. In point of fact, the name Savannah is only an altered form of the tribal name. See Hawkins, p. 83; Thomas S. Woodward, *Reminiscences of the Creek, or Muscogee, Indians*, p. 18.
33. For descriptions of these sacred metal plates long preserved in the Tuckabatchee town on Tallapoosa River, see Adair, p. 178; Pickett, vol. I, p. 84. The Reverend R. M. Loughridge saw these plates exhibited at the annual Busk of the Tuckabatchee town in the Indian Territory, August 1852. Schoolcraft, vol. V, p. 660.
34. The principal Hitchitee town in Hawkins's time was on the Georgia side of the river below Oswichee Bend.
35. On the upper waters of the Alabama and Coosa, and on the lower waters of the Chattahoochee and Tallapoosa, there were interspersed among the towns

speaking the pure Muscogee dialect some towns that spoke a broken-down dialect of Choctaw. The vocabulary was largely ancient Choctaw, but the grammatical structure did not differ much from pure Creek. The white traders and Indian country men called this mongrel dialect "the Stinkard speech." Doubtless the term "Stinkard" was a translation of some derisive name given to this form of speech by the towns that spoke pure Muscogee. Bartram (p. 461) gives a list of the towns speaking the Stinkard dialect in 1776. The Alabamas, Coosawdas, and Hitchitees, probably also the Coosas, Coushacs, Abekas, and Abekoochees, spoke the Stinkard dialect.

36. [Stiggins is in error here. The Hitchitees are considered the oldest group in the Creek Confederacy. Some of them drifted south after the American Revolution and joined with others to form the Seminole tribe. Brown and Owens, pp. 145-46.]

37. The word Se-man-o-le, properly pronounced with four syllables and not with three, as all our dictionaries mark it, is a Muscogee word, and means "he that goes apart"—"separatist." The Seminole language is essentially Muscogee, with many Hitchitee, that is to say, ancient Choctaw, words in its vocabulary.

38. [Hudson (pp. 202-11) states that the southeastern Indian form of government can best be described as a series of chiefdoms, a chiefdom being a type of political organization standing midway between decentralized tribal governments such as those of the Iroquois and the Navajos and the centralized governments of the Aztecs and the Incas.]

39. [The terms *chief* and *micco* (Creek) are used interchangeably in most writings about southeastern Indians. Spaniards called chiefs *caciques*, an Arawak Indian word for *chief*.]

40. [The Creeks acquired rum from traders, who in some instances got the Indians drunk and cheated them out of their deerskins. No doubt they did drink immoderately, but whether, as Hudson suggests (p. 441), rum was the cause of their ills or simply a concomitant of contact with whites is debatable. According to his son, Stiggins himself drank heavily at times but abstained for months or even years.]

41. The famous black drink was a decoction of the leaves of the *Ilex cassine* or *Ilex vomitoria*, a species of holly which is found in the coast plain region from southeastern Virginia to the Colorado Valley in Texas. Charles Thomas Mohr, *Plant Life of Alabama*, p. 653; Alice Lounsberry, *Southern Wild Flowers and Trees*, p. 315; A. W. Chapman, *Flora of the Southern United States*. The white people call it Yopon or Yupon. The Creek name of the shrub is Usse. The black drink is Usse pusse.

42. This is true of some of the towns only. The old Coosa town, celebrated in the oldest historical records of the eighteenth century as a peace town, was beyond reasonable doubt the same Coosa visited by De Soto in 1540. Barcia, p. 35; Davila Padilla, p. 205; *Memoria de Juan de la Vandera* in Buckingham Smith's *Coleccion de varios documentos para la Historia de la Florida*, p. 19. Tallassee and Tuckabatchee on the Tallapoosa, and Cusseta on the Chattahoochee, were very old towns. On the other hand, Tuscaloosa on the Alabama, Talla-

muchassee, Ullibahali, and other towns that were flourishing in the heart of the Creek country in De Soto's time disappeared, at least in name, from the lists in later times.

43. [In this digression Stiggins seems to be judging the Creeks by the behavioral standards of the white world. His evaluation here is inconsistent with his attitude elsewhere in his writing. No doubt he experienced frustration and bitterness as he observed the final breakup of Creek society after the Creek War.]

44. This is the solemn religious festival celebrated annually by each town on the ripening of the green corn. White people living among the Creeks called it the Green Corn Dance. The proper form of the word is Posketa, which means "a fast." Hawkins gives an elaborate account of the Posketa as it was celebrated by the people of the Tuckabatchee town (p. 75). The punishment for adultery is described by many writers: Hawkins, Pope, Bossu, and others.

45. [The word *loke* is apparently not translatable. The word in the bracketed space could not be read by the editor.]

46. [Hudson gives very much the same account of Creek marriage customs (pp. 196-202). Hudson does not list Stiggins in his bibliography. His information came from Swanton, Tuggle, Adair.]

47. This is a Creek war title which means "war leader." *Tustenuggee emathla* means "warrior of the highest rank." I fancy that it is related to the Choctaw *emathle,* "full-grown man," which was sometimes used as a war-name by the Choctaws and Chickasaws.

48. This is one of the four sacred medicinal plants, the

virtues of which were miraculously revealed to the Creeks while they were removing eastward from their original seats beyond the Mississippi. *Mikko-hoyanecha* means "chief's purgative." It is said to be a species of willow—perhaps *Salix tristus*. Brinton, p. 11.

49. Another of the sacred plants. The word *awotichka* means "emetic." Hawkins says (p. 78), "It is a very bitter root and has the effect of intoxicating and maddening."

50. The Creek name for the Almighty is Hesaket-emisse, "the giver of breath." The Alabama name for God is Aba-mingo, "the ruler above." The Choctaw is Chito-kaka, "the great one."

51. The names and number of the clans differ somewhat as given by different authorities. The list furnished Gatschet by Judge Stidham of the Indian Territory comprehends twenty-eight, including those extinct and those still existing. Gatschet, p. 155. The list printed in L. H. Morgan's *Ancient Society* (p. 161), was furnished by the Reverend R. M. Loughridge, and gives thirty gentes or "clans." Henry Frieland Buckner names only sixteen, but he does not aim to furnish the complete list. *Maskoke Grammar*, p. 59.

52. *Hotululke*. This is the clan to which belonged the first Sehoy, maternal ancestor of the McGillivrays, Weatherfords, Tates, and other families of mixed blood in Alabama.

[Half bloods, or mixed bloods, of white and Creek extraction played important roles in tribal affairs, especially in dealings with the whites. Big Warrior and Menewa were also of mixed blood.

Legend says the Wind clan was so named because a

great fog once shrouded all the Creek people, and the first group to emerge into the clearing wind became the Wind clan. W. E. S. Folsom-Dickerson, *The White Path* (San Antonio, Texas: Naylor Co., 1965), p. 8.]

53. [There were certain towns among the Creeks known as peace, or white, towns, set aside for refuge, e.g., Coweta. The biblical reference is Genesis 9:6.]
54. Wasassa was the name given by the Creeks to the Osage Indians. So says Buckner (p. 60). But Stiggins's statement is probably correct.
55. This agent was Colonel John Stuart who came to Georgia with Governor Oglethorpe in 1733. He was appointed British superintendent of the southern Indians in 1763, and was still superintendent when the Revolutionary War began. He adhered to the Crown and was instrumental in turning the Cherokees and Creeks against the revolted colonies.
56. Colonel Thomas Tate was one of Stuart's deputies among the Creeks during the Revolution. He is said to have trained Creek Indians at Fort Toulouse and led them against the Americans in Georgia. Tate was the first husband of Sehoy McGillivray, daughter of Lachlan McGillivray, a Scotch trader among the Creeks before the war. Sehoy was a sister of Alexander McGillivray, the celebrated leader of the Creeks during the war and after. Colonel Tate died during the war and was buried at Cusseta. After his death Sehoy married Charles Weatherford, another white trader, and became the mother of William Weatherford, the Red Eagle, who led the Creeks in the assault on Fort Mims.

    Woodward says that Tate's first name was John (p. 59).

Abram Mordecai, a Jewish trader among the Creeks, is authority for the statement that Tate during the War of the Revolution drilled squads of Tories and Indians at Alabama (or Ekon-chatte), a town of the Alabamas on the bluff just below the present site of Montgomery. Matthew Powers Blue, *City Directory and History of Montgomery, Alabama*, p. 5.

57. John Galphin was a brother of the better-known George Galphin, one of the Scotch traders who took the side of the patriots in the Revolutionary War. John adopted the cause of the British and went off among the Indians. Leslie was another Scotch trader among the Creeks. He was the father of Alexander Leslie, the half-breed for whom Fort Lashley near Talladega was named. Woodward, pp. 61, 62.

58. The Great Mortar of the Hillabee town was a famous chieftain before and during the Revolution. Adair often speaks of him as a man of mark.

[For a full discussion of Great Mortar's political role in Creek-Colonial affairs see Owen, pp. 755-758.]

59. The incident here related belongs to the spring of the year 1782, when General Wayne had the town of Savannah, then in possession of the British troops, closely invested. A body of three hundred Creek Indians under the chief Guristersigo attempted to penetrate the American lines for the purpose of reinforcing the British garrison. The historians of Georgia agree in saying that the Indians were dispersed and driven back to the Creek nation. Hugh M'Call, *The History of Georgia*, vol. II, p. 410; William Bacon Stevens, *A History of Georgia*, vol. II, p. 286; Charles C. Jones, Jr., *The History of Georgia*, vol. II, p. 512. For a full account see Henry

Lee, *Memoirs of the War in the Southern Department,* p. 556.

60. The year was 1790, and the seat of government was New York. Here was concluded the first treaty between the United States and the Creek Indians. General Henry Knox, secretary of war, was the commissioner for the Government of the U.S. and Alexander McGillivray for the Creeks. [A master diplomat, Alexander McGillivray held the title of head chief and principal warrior of the Creek nation from 1783 to 1793. For a biography see John Walton Caughey, *McGillivray of the Creeks* (Norman: University of Oklahoma Press, 1938).]
61. The "great beloved man" (Iste-achaka-hlokko) was General Washington.
62. The limits established by the Treaty of Fort Jackson 1814, and subsequent treaties to the year 1832.
63. The old Mad Dog, Tustenuggee Hacho, was principal chief of the Tuckabatchees before the Big Warrior, Tustenuggee Hlokko. Schoolcraft, vol. V, p. 254. He died in 1811.
64. The Creek name for an American of the white race to this day is Wachena.
65. The name of Fort Louis de la Louisiane, built by the French at Mobile in 1710, was changed first in 1720 to Fort Conde, afterwards by the English in 1763 to Fort Charlotte. Hamilton, *Colonial Mobile,* pp. 70, 86, 177.

    [Fort Charlotte is now called Fort Conde again. The city of Mobile has partially reconstructed it, and it is open to the public.]
66. The relation of the capture of Mobile in 1780 by Don

Bernardo de Galvez, Spanish governor of Louisiana, is given in full detail in Hamilton's *Colonial Mobile* (p. 253); but Stiggins adds a new chapter to the record in this story of the unsuccessful attempt of the Great Mortar and his Creek warriors to succor their British friends beleaguered in Mobile.

67. The first agent of the United States for the Creeks was Dr. James White, appointed in 1787; the second was James Seagrore, appointed in 1791. Colonel Benjamin Hawkins of North Carolina was the third agent, appointed in 1797.

    [Hawkins negotiated the Treaty of Coleraine (1796) with the Creeks and served as U.S. agent of the Creeks and general superintendent of the southern tribes 1796-1816. For his biography see Merritt B. Pound, *Benjamin Hawkins—Indian Agent* (Athens: University of Georgia Press, 1951).]

68. [Stiggins may be referring to Tecumseh's brother, Tenskwatawa, known as the Shawnee prophet. Thomas L. McKenney said, "He was a powerful orator, . . . but his words were those of Tecumseh." He had been a "boasting, swaggering drunk" until 1805 when he "found religion and became a mystic." James D. Horan, *The McKenney-Hall Portrait Gallery of American Indians* (New York: Crown, 1972), p. 156. The prophet who accompanied Tecumseh on his visit to the southern tribes was also a kinsman, called Seekaboo.]

69. These murders, committed in 1812 near the mouth of the Ohio by the Coosawdas under the leadership of Tuskegee Tustenuggee while they were returning from the visit to the Shawnees, are often confounded with

the murders committed the same year at the mouth of Luck River, Tennessee. For an account of the punishment of these murders, see *American State Papers, Documents, Legislative and Executive, of the Congress of the United States*, Class II, Indian Affairs, vol. I, pp. 837, 841, 843.

70. Tecumseh visited the Creeks in October 1811. Most of the histories of the time place his visit a year later.

[Tecumseh was of Creek descent, both his parents having been born at Sauwanogee, a Shawnee town on the Tallapoosa River, where they lived until 1790. R. S. Cotterill, *The Southern Indians* (Norman: University of Oklahoma Press, 1954), p. 167.]

71. The comet was visible during the summer of 1811. The first earthquake shock that convinced the Creeks that Tecumseh had "put his foot down" came on the night of December 16, 1811. The shock was accompanied by loud subterranean noises. At Nashville chimneys were thrown down. At Pensacola houses creaked, doors and windows were shaken. On January 12, 1812, there was another violent earthquake. This is the one that wrecked the town of New Madrid, Missouri. On January 23 a slight shock was felt at New Orleans and Pensacola. Slight oscillations were felt at New Orleans, St. Stephens, and other places in the South on February 4. These continued for several days. No wonder that the Creeks believed in the power and the prophecies of Tecumseh.

72. [Big Warrior (Tustennugge Hlocco), head chief and speaker of the Creek Nation during the Creek War, played a pivotal role in U.S.-Creek affairs. When he

died in 1824, his obituary appeared in Niles Register. Woodward said that Big Warrior was the largest man he ever saw among the Creeks and that he was almost as spotted as a leopard. Thomas S. Woodward, *Woodward's Reminiscences of the Creek, or Muscogee, Indians* (Montgomery, 1859; reprint, Alabama Book Store, Tuscaloosa, and Birmingham Book Exchange, Birmingham, 1939), p. 116.]

73. [Owen points out that Big Warrior's peace party was in the minority among the Creeks (five peace towns and twenty-nine hostile or Red Stick towns) and that Big Warrior acted out of loyalty to the U.S., rather than fear of U.S. retaliation, in trying to subdue the hostiles (vol. II, p. 740).]

74. [Owen states that Isaacs was persistently loyal to the United States and was executed in 1813 by the hostile Creeks because of this. Owen makes no mention of Isaacs as a prophet (vol. II, p. 746).]

75. The ancient town of Tuckabatchee was on the right bank of the Tallapoosa River at the great bend four miles south of the modern manufacturing town of Tallassee. The Tuckabatchee plantation of Dr. Robert J. Ware, a wealthy and representative citizen of Montgomery County, before the late war included the Tuckabatchee Bend and the site of the old Indian town. Immediately opposite Tuckabatchee, on the left bank of the river, just above the mouth of Yufaupe Creek, was the Indian town of Tallassee, called Big Tallassee to distinguish it from Little Tallassee four miles above the falls of the Coosa at Wetumpka. Here Alexander McGillivray lived. It is well to bear in mind the fact that

the Tuckabatchees were friendly to the whites. The Tallassees belonged to the Red Sticks or hostile Indians.

[The site of Little Tallassee, also called Apple Grove, is marked with a rose quartz marker beside the Thelma Baptist Church, Wallsboro Crossroads, near Wetumpka, Alabama. Lachlan McGillivray, the Scottish trader who married Sehoy of the Wind clan, started a plantation here in 1740. Their son Alexander McGillivray was born here.]

76. Pickett says that David Francis, father of the half-breed Josiah Francis, was a trader of Scotch and Irish descent (vol. II, p. 245).

77. [Stiggins's numbers here are unclear. It seems likely that the 4,800 refers to the total number of Lower Town hostiles. See Swanton, pp. 421-57, for a detailed discussion of Creek population. McGillivray about 1790 estimated the number of gunmen for the Creek nation at between 5,000 and 6,000 and the entire population at about 20,000. The U.S. census of 1833, taken at the time of the removal to the west, showed the Lower Creek towns had a population of 8,552 people. Hudson, p. 457.]

78. Joe Marshall was a half-breed Indian of Cusseta. His father was an Englishman who lived at the falls of the Chattahoochee, where Columbus now stands. The writer of these notes as he records the name of Joseph Marshall draws up from the deepest wells of memory childish recollections of Ben Marshall, but especially of "Aunt Polly Marshall" as the children and some of the grown folk of her acquaintance liked to call her. She was so good and kind and true. These two were son and daughter of old Joe Marshall. Woodward, p. 114.

79. This creek was called Okfuskee, until after the Treaty of Fort Jackson, when it was made the southern boundary line of the Creek nation south of the Tallapoosa.

80. [Sam Moniac, half-blooded brother-in-law of Francis, described High-headed Jim's prophetic seizures: "He shook hands with me, and immediately began to tremble and jerk . . . and the very calves of his legs would be convulsed, and he would get entirely out of breath. . . . This practice was introduced in May or June last by the Prophet Francis." H. S. Halbert and T. H. Ball, *The Creek War of 1813 and 1814*, Frank L. Owsley, Jr., ed. (University: University of Alabama Press, 1969), p. 92.]

81. [High-headed Jim, or Jim Boy, chief of the Autossees, was also known by several Indian names; see note 83. In the Creek war he fought with the hostiles. Later, however, he raised troops and fought with the Americans in the Seminole wars, with the understanding that his family and his property would be protected. He returned home to find his property destroyed and his family gone, sent west in the removal. He died in the Creek Nation (west) in 1851. Jim Boy was described as a remarkably handsome man, over six feet tall, with a commanding air. Owen, vol. II, p. 747.]

82. The Cut Off in Clarke County is a stream connecting the waters of the Tombigbee and the Alabama, four miles above the junction.

83. The date of the battle of Burnt Corn Creek is July 27, 1813. The fullest and most accurate of the published accounts of this battle is to be found in H. S. Halbert and T. H. Ball's *Creek War of 1813 and 1814* (p. 125). Stiggins's

relation agrees with this in the main and may be taken as the Indian account of the fight. Other authorities are Pickett's *Alabama*, vol. II, p. 256; Alexander Beaufort Meek's *Romantic Passages in Southwestern History*, p. 244; J. F. H. Claiborne's *Life and Times of Gen. Sam Dale*, p. 72. According to Stiggins, the leader of the Creeks at Burnt Corn was not Peter McQueen, as the other authors relate, but Cusseta Tustenuggee or High-headed Jim, otherwise called Jim Boy, who was afterwards a conspicuous actor in the Creek revolt in 1835. Colonel William H. Sparks, who knew Jim Boy in 1835, describes him as a man of herculean proportions. "He was six feet eight inches in height, and in every way admirably proportioned." He calls him Tuskegee Tustenuggee. *The Memories of Fifty Years*, p. 478.

84. [A popularly written book about Weatherford entitled *Red Eagle and the Wars with the Creek Indians in Alabama* appeared in 1878 (New York: Dodd and Mead). The author, George Cary Eggleston, portrayed Weatherford in much the same light as Stiggins does: an unwilling participant in the Creek War, albeit the mastermind of Indian strategy.]
85. Fort Pierce was a smaller stockade about two miles from Fort Mims, named for two brothers Pierce who lived hard by.
86. Woodward calls him Paddy Welsh.
87. The full form is Enah-homahtah, hohle hopoyah, which means "he that seeks to be the first in battle."
88. The name is pure Muscogee and not Alabama: Ku-lechah, "he that kindles a fire."
89. Fort Sinquefield was about five miles southeast from

Grove Hill, the present county seat of Clarke County. The fullest account of the attack on Fort Sinquefield on the morning of September 2, 1813, three days after the destruction of Fort Mims, will be found in Halbert and Ball, p. 184. The published accounts say that Josiah Francis, whose Indian name was Alikche Hacho, the Mud Doctor, was the leader of the Indians in this assault. I incline to the opinion that Stiggins has given a true relation of the matter.

90. Ekon-achaka, the Holy Ground town, was situated on a high bluff on the left bank of the Alabama, about two miles north of the present Whitehall Station in Lowndes County. Pickett, following the earlier authorities, asserts that the town was built by Weatherford. It is probable that Stiggins's statement is trustworthy, namely that it was built and fortified by Francis and his Alabama adherents. Meek (p. 279) asserts that here the council house of the Alabamas was situated; but this may well be doubted. It was a new and hastily constructed village.

91. The date of the capture and destruction of Ekon-achaka is December 23, 1813.

92. The story of Weatherford's famous leap from the top of the bluff into the river is told by Meek, Pickett, and others with varying detail. Woodward (p. 100) attempts to discredit the story, but Pickett derived his information from Weatherford himself. Stiggins, who was closely related to the Weatherfords, must have gotten his information at firsthand. His account may be accepted as true in all important particulars.

93. [Owen considers Francis one of the most important

chiefs and the greatest prophet in the Creek nation during this time. He points out that "Francis was no more guilty than other Creeks for massacres during the war and whom Gen. Jackson did not punish" (p. 745). In London, Francis, who spoke English as well as Spanish and Muscogee, was royally received, made a colonel in the British army, presented with a diamond-studded snuff box and a tomahawk set with gold (p. 744).]

94. The McQueens were half bloods, sons of old James McQueen, a white man of Tallassee. Woodward, p. 110.

95. [Owen says the battle of Autossee was fought November 29, 1813. "It . . . represents the principal contribution of Georgia to the defense of the Mississippi Territory in the Creek War." General John Floyd commanded the Georgia militia (vol. I, pp. 83-84).]

96. Perhaps this is for echo-sikne-wakna, "the spike-horn deer's lair."

97. William McGillivray, a half-blooded son of Daniel McDonald, a Scotch trader who took the name of McGillivray after the death of Alexander McGillivray in 1793. Woodward calls him "Bit Nose Billy McGillivray."

98. Stiggins and Woodward agree in the statement that Weatherford took part in only three battles of the war: Fort Mims, Holy Ground, and Autossee.

99. [The battle of Calabee took place January 27, 1814, about seven miles from Tuskegee. The Creeks had assembled a large force of about 1,800 warriors, many without guns, armed only with war club and bows and arrows. They were no match for the Georgia militia

with bayonets and cannons. Owen, vol. I, p. 190.]

100. This account of the fight on the Alabama River in which Lieutenant Joseph M. Wilcox was killed differs widely from the relation of the events given to Pickett by G. W. Creagh of Clarke County. The story as told by Pickett cannot be accurate because, according to that, no survivor of Wilcox's little band was left to tell the story. Stiggins also must be wrong in the statement that Wilcox was killed by Paddy Walsh and his gang after the battle of Calabee Swamp. Wilcox and his men were killed January 15, 1814. Pickett says February, but that is in error. The Calabee fight came off twelve days after Wilcox's death January 27, 1814.

101. [The manuscript abruptly ends here. See Wyman's Introduction.]

Works Cited in Wyman's Notes

[Wyman gave little publishing information on his sources. The editor has been able to identify most sources but possibly not always in the edition used by Wyman. Reprints are indicated in brackets.]

Adair, James. *The History of the American Indians*. London: E. and C. Dilly, 1775. [Nashville: Blue and Gray Press, 1971.]

Barcia Carballido y Zuñiga, Andres Gonzalez de. *Ensayo cronológico para la historia general de la Florida*. Madrid, 1723. [Westport, Conn.: Greenwood, 1970.]

Bartram, William. *Travels Through North and South Carolina, Georgia, East and West Florida*. Philadelphia, 1791. London, 1792, 1794. [New Haven: Yale University Press, 1958.]

Blue, Matthew Powers. *City Directory and History of Montgomery, Alabama*. Montgomery, Ala.: T. C. Bingham, 1878.

Bossu, Jean-Bernard. *Nouveaux voyages dans l'Amerique Septentrionale*. Amsterdam, Changuion, 1777. [*Travels in the Interior of North America, 1751-1762*. Translated and edited by Seymour Feiler. Norman: University of Oklahoma Press, 1962.]

Boston. Massachusetts Historical-Genealogical Society Library. "Sketch of the history of the Creek Indians" made for General Henry Knox by Alexander McGillivray, 1790.

Brinton, Daniel G. "National Legend of the Chahta-Muskokee Tribes." *American Historical Magazine*, February 1870.

Buckner, Henry Frieland. *Maskoke Grammar*.

Chapman, A. W. *Flora of the Southern United States*. New York: Ivison, Phinney, 1860.

Claiborne, J. F. H. *Life and Times of Gen. Sam Dale, the Mississippi Partisan*. New York: Harper, 1860.

Davila Padilla, Fray Agustin. *Historia de la Fundacion y Discurso de la Provincia de Santiago de Mexico*. Brussels, 1625.

Elvas, Gentleman of. *Narrative of the Gentleman of Elvas*. Translated by Richard Hakluyt. London, 1609. [*Narratives of De Soto in the Conquest of Florida*. Translated by Buckingham Smith. Gainesville, Fla.: Palmetto Books, 1968.]

Gallatin, Albert. *A Synopsis of the Indian Tribes Within the United States East of the Rocky Mountains*. American Antiquarian Society Transactions, Archaeologica Americana, vol. 2. Cambridge, 1836.

Gatschet, Albert S. *A Migration Legend of the Creek Indians*. Brinton's Library of Aboriginal American Literature, vol 1. Philadelphia, 1884. [New York: AMS Press, 1969.]

Halbert, H. S., and Ball, T. H. *The Creek War of 1813 and 1814*. Chicago: Donohue and Henneberry; Montgomery: White, Woodruff, and Fowler, 1895. [Ed. Frank L. Owsley, Jr., University: University of Alabama Press, 1969.]

Hamilton, Peter J. *Colonial Mobile*. Boston: Houghton, Mifflin, 1897. [Ed. Charles G. Summersell, Birmingham:

University of Alabama Press, 1976.]
Hamilton, Peter J., and Owen, Thomas McAdory, eds. *Tatum's Journal*. Transactions of the Alabama Historical Society, vol. 2. Tuscaloosa, 1852-55.
Hawkins, Benjamin. *A Sketch of the Creek Country*. Georgia Historical Society Collections, vol. 3. Savannah, 1848. [Americus, Ga.: Americus Book Co., 1938.]
Holcombe, Hosea. *History of the Baptists in Alabama*. Philadelphia: King and Baird, 1840.
Jones, Charles C., Jr. *The History of Georgia*. Boston: Houghton, Mifflin, 1883.
La Harpe, Bernard de. *Journal Historique de l'éstablissement des Francais à la Louisiane*. New Orleans, 1831. [*Historical Journal of the Establishment of the French in Louisiana. Historical collections of Louisiana*. Edited by Benjamin F. French. New York: 1851.]
Lee, Henry. *Memoirs of the War in the Southern Department*. Philadelphia: Bradford and Inskeep, 1812. New edition, 1869. [New York: New York Times, 1969.]
Lounsberry, Alice. *Southern Wild Flowers and Trees*. New York: Frederick A. Stokes, 1901.
Lowrie, Walter, et al., ed. *The American State Papers, Documents, Legislative, and Executive of the Congress of the United States*. 39 vols. Indian Affairs, vol. 1. Washington: Government Printing Office, 1832-61.
M'Call, Hugh. *The History of Georgia*. 2 vols. Savannah: William T. Williams, 1811, 1816. [Atlanta: Caldwell, 1909.]
Meek, Alexander Beaufort. *Romantic Passages in Southwestern History*. 4th ed. New York, Mobile: S. H. Goetzel, 1857.
Milford, Louis Le Clerc. *Memoire ou coup-d'oeil rapide sur*

mes differens voyages et mon sejour dans la nation Creck. Paris, 1802. [*Memoirs, or a Quick Glance at My Various Travels and My Sojourn in the Creek Nation.* Trans. and ed. by Ben C. McCary. Savannah, Ga.: The Beehive Press, 1972.]

Missionary Herald, vol. 24.

Mohr, Charles Theodore. *Plant Life of Alabama.* Washington: U.S. Department of Agriculture; Geological Survey of Alabama; 1901. [West Germany: Verlag Von J. Cramer, 1969.]

Moore, Clarence B. "Certain Aboriginal Remains of the Alabama River." *Journal of the Academy of Natural Sciences of Philadelphia* 11 (1899):289-337.

Morgan, Lewis Henry. *Ancient Society.* Chicago: C. H. Kerr, 1877. [Cambridge: Belknap Press of Harvard University Press, 1910.]

Pénicaut, André. "Relation de Pénicaut" in Pierre Margry's *Découvertes et Etablissements des Francais dans l'Ouest et dans le Sud de l'Amérique Septentrionale*, vol 5. Paris, 1883.

Pickett, Albert James. *History of Alabama and Incidentally of Georgia and Mississippi, from the Earliest Period.* 2 vols. Charleston: Walker and James, 1851. [Birmingham; Webb Book Co., 1900.]

Romans, Bernard. *A Concise Natural History of East and West Florida.* New York: 1775. [Facsimile reproduction of 1775 ed. Gainesville: University of Florida Press, 1962.]

Schoolcraft, Henry Rowe. *Historical and Statistical Information Respecting the History, Conditions, and Prospects of the Indian Tribes of the U.S.* 6 vols. Philadelphia: Lippincott, 1851-57.

Sparks, William Henry. *The Memories of Fifty Years.* 4th ed.

Philadelphia, n.d.

Stevens, William Bacon. *A History of Georgia*. 2 vols.

Vandera, Juan de la. *Memoria de Juan de la Vandera* in Buckingham Smith's *Coleccion de vàrios documentos para la Historia de la Florida*.

Willett, William Marinus. *A Narrative of the Military Actions of Colonel Marinus Willett*. New York: G. and C. and H. Carvill, 1831.

Woodward, Thomas S. *Woodward's Reminiscences of the Creek, or Muscogee, Indians*. Montgomery: Barrett and Wimbish, 1859. [Tuscaloosa: Alabama Book Store, 1939.]

INDEX

The decorative device used throughout the book was reproduced from a prehistoric shell gorget with rattlesnake design.